Just a Minute

**Sixty Seconds a Day
with the Gospels**

Fr. Vincent Serpa, O.P.

San Diego
2011

Published by Catholic Answers
2020 Gillespie Way
El Cajon, California 92020

619-387-7200

www.catholic.com

Cover by Devin Schadt
Interior design by Russell Design

Printed in the United States of America

ISBN 978-1-933919-48-5

For my mother and my sister.

Introduction

A minute-long sound bite seems like such an insignificant attempt at communication. It might even seem unwise or a waste of effort. But then, using uneducated fishermen to initiate the communication of the most significant news in the history of the human race might seem unwise or a waste of effort as well. Yet these were the people the Lord handpicked. The daily Gospel selections that the Liturgy of the Word gives us are, we believe, the very words he wants us to hear. To reflect on them even for just one minute is to allow oneself to listen to him. It is God speaking to us in time.

When one considers the significant events that occur within sixty seconds, one is forced to conclude that the minute isn't so lowly after all. Human beings are conceived within the space of a minute, and they can die within that time as well. It takes less than a minute for a bishop to lay his hands on the head of a man to make him a priest. Marriage vows take place within sixty seconds. But most of all, the Lord breathed his last in a matter of seconds and transformed the human race forever.

The Liturgy of the Hours sanctifies time. At any minute throughout the day people are praising God through the liturgy somewhere in the world. To spend a minute listening to the Lord and reflecting on his message can not only lift our spirits; it can become an occasion of prayer. I have found this to be true in writing these reflections. I hope is it true for those who listen to them on the radio and also those who read them here. My thanks to Erik Gustafson for his many hours spent reading and tweaking them for publication. I'm also indebted to him for engineering the minute for broadcast over the years and more recently to Matthew Tuszynski.

—Fr. Vincent Serpa, O.P.
   April 26, 2011
   Tuesday in the Octave of Easter

Sunday, Octave Day of Christmas
Luke 2:16–21

The shepherds found Mary and Joseph and the baby lying in the manger. The angel's message to her, the birth event itself, and the reaction of those who witnessed it were not lost on Mary. All her life she treasured things in her heart that no one else would ever be able to treasure. God chose her alone from all eternity to conceive in her own body the Redeemer of the human race. She alone nursed God at her breast. Her life gives the word *unique* new meaning. To dismiss her as nothing special—other than the Mother of Jesus—is to disregard him and who he is. What an insult to insinuate that anyone who would be his Mother could be anything but very, very special!

And so we honor her today for who she is, Mary, the Mother of God—the Mother of us all. If there has ever been a Mother for all people, it has to be her.

JANUARY 2, 2012

John 1:19–28

John the Baptist stated quite openly, "I am not the Christ!" Well, was he Elijah? "I am not," he said. Are you a prophet? "No." he exclaimed. Those who questioned him were sent by the Pharisees and needed to take back some definite information about him. So they pressed him further: "Why are you baptizing if you are not the Christ and not Elijah?" John responded that he was baptizing with water, but there was one unknown to them who was coming after him whose sandal strap he was not worthy to undo.

They were getting nowhere fast, because even though they asked him who he was, they really didn't want to know, did they? They wanted information that would satisfy the Pharisees who were putting pressure on them. Often we ask the Lord, "Why?" when we don't like our present situation. We don't really want to know why; we just want our way. If those people had only known the significance of their questions, they would have been able to witness God's presence in their midst. This is true of our "whys?" as well.

John 1:29–34

John the Baptist saw Jesus coming toward him and exclaimed, "Behold, the Lamb of God. . . ." he explained that he did not know Jesus until he saw the Spirit come down and remain upon him. John, of course, had been in the desert for twenty years, so he wouldn't have recognized his cousin unless the Spirit pointed him out. But John knew that his whole mission in life was to prepare the people for Jesus' coming by offering them a baptism of repentance. So it was with great delight and satisfaction that he finally saw Jesus, the person for whom he had been living his life.

Our baptism, of course, was not a baptism of repentance but an initiation into the life of Jesus. We are not preparing for the coming of the Messiah. He has come and has made us his disciples. But we only know this by the gift of faith that the Holy Spirit has given us. We haven't seen him with our eyes—yet. But one day, like John, we will see him for whom we have been living our lives!

John 1:35–42

John the Baptist, with two of his disciples, looked up and, seeing Jesus pass by, exclaimed, "Behold, the Lamb of God." When John's disciples began to follow Jesus, he turned to them and asked what they were looking for. They answered, "Rabbi, where are you staying?" He told them to come and see. So they spent the day with him. Andrew, one of the two, left and told his brother, Simon, "We have found the Messiah." So he brought him to meet Jesus, who changed Simon's name to Cephas, which means Peter.

This is our story, yours and mine. Before your baptism, someone (probably your parents) recognized Jesus as the Savior and wanted you to be his follower. And with your great meeting with Jesus at your baptism you received your name. People actually know who you are because you have been baptized into Jesus Christ. So you are a Christian. This is who you are.

JANUARY 5, 2012

John 1:43–51

When Jesus told Philip to follow him, Philip told Nathaniel that they had found the one the prophets had spoken about. Nathaniel replied, "Can anything good come from Nazareth?" "Come and see." Philip replied. "Here is a true child of Israel. There is no duplicity in him." Jesus said when he saw Nathaniel. Nathaniel wanted to know how Jesus knew him. Jesus replied that he had seen him in the past. Nathaniel was bowled over. Jesus promised that he was to experience far greater things than the fact that he had known him intimately from afar.

Nathaniel was impressed with the knowledge that Jesus had of him without his knowing about it. It was knowledge that Jesus couldn't have had from merely human means. He has this same knowledge of you. Just think of your own private history. How far back do you remember? Do you recall the secrets you had that you kept to yourself? Well, they weren't as secret as you thought. He was there. He knows you like the back of his hand. And as with Nathaniel, he has far greater things for you in store.

Luke 3:23–38

Luke gives us the genealogy of Jesus from Adam to St. Joseph, his foster father. A knowledge of one's ancestors is supposed to give us some idea of who we are. I'm told that my ancestors on my maternal grandmother's side were winemakers. It's a pleasant piece of information, but it doesn't have any bearing on my day-to-day existence that I can see. But somewhere in my background, many generations ago, a person accepted the teachings of Jesus Christ from the Catholic Church, which has made this time between you and me possible.

Obviously, ancestors matter. The ancestors of Jesus mattered because the Messiah was to be of the house of David. Even though St. Joseph was not his biological father, the ancestral line was received from the man who was the head of the family. Jesus was of the house of David. But more importantly, he is the Savior who made his home in the world, has cleansed us with the healing waters of baptism and feeds us with himself. This is how important his genealogy is to us.

John 2:1–11

Jesus was at a wedding in Cana in Galilee. When the wine ran short, his Mother told him, "They have no wine." Jesus asked what this had to do with him, because he had not yet begun his public life. She responded simply by telling the servers to do whatever he requested. Jesus then changed six stone jars of water into the celebration's finest wine. At this, his public life began.

Certainly Jesus could have worked the miracle secretly before even the servers knew. But he chose to let his Mother ask him. In deference to her he began his public life. The chemistry between Jesus and Mary required few words. Such chemistry, of course, still exists.

Jesus showed us many times that he wants us to intercede for each other, because it is the way of love. We don't compete with him when we pray to the Father for each other. All our prayers go through Jesus anyway. So we delight that he gives mere humans this privilege.

First Sunday of Ordinary Time
Year B • Matthew 2:1–12

Astrologers from the east inquired in Jerusalem about the newborn king of the Jews. They had observed his star and come to pay him homage. Greatly disturbed, King Herod asked them to inform him of the child's location if they should find him, so that he might offer homage also. After leaving him, they once again observed the star and followed it to the manger where Jesus lay. After prostrating themselves and honoring him, they offered him gifts of gold, frankincense, and myrrh. After receiving a warning in a dream, they avoided Herod on their return home.

The astrologers saw Jesus as one to whom they owed homage. Herod saw him as nothing but a threat to his power and to his having things his way. This scenario still exists today. Some pay him homage, while others see him and his Church as a threat to having things their own way. But in the end we will all know him as the loving Redeemer that he is.

Feast of the Baptism of the Lord

Monday of the First Week
of Ordinary Time • Mark 1:7–11

Jesus appeared before John the Baptist, asking to be baptized. John immediately objected. "I need to be baptized by you," he said. But Jesus assured him that for this occasion it had to be as it was the will of his Father. So John consented. When Jesus stepped out of the water after John baptized him, the heavens opened and the Holy Spirit, in the form of a dove, hovered over him as the Father announced, "This is my beloved Son. My favor rests on him." This interchange with John and the voice of the Father confirmed John as the last prophet of the Old Law and the beginning of the Law's fulfillment in Jesus.

This demonstrates that the fulfillment of the Father's will consists in Jesus redeeming the likes of you and me . . . and everyone else.

Tuesday of the First Week
of Ordinary Time • Mark 1:21–28

Jesus entered the synagogue in Capernaum on the Sabbath and astonished the people with his teaching because he spoke with authority. The scribes had tended only to repeat what others had said before them without delving much into the meaning of what was said. A man with an unclean spirit cried out in recognition of who Jesus was. "Quiet! Come out of him!" Jesus ordered, and the unclean spirit left him. This impressed the people all the more and his fame spread throughout the area.

Today his Church speaks with that same authority, the power of which is evident even in the threat it poses to those who revile it. It wields his power over evil as it has for over two thousand years. It's a power that has been best expressed through the sacrifices of its saints and the blood of its martyrs.

Wednesday of the First Week
of Ordinary Time • Mark 1:29–39

Jesus entered the house of Simon and Andrew, where Simon's mother-in-law lay ill with fever. He approached her, and as he took her hand the fever left her and she served them. After sunset the whole town was gathered at the door, where he drove out demons and cured the sick. Early the next morning while Jesus was at prayer, Simon and the others came to him with the words, "Everyone is looking for you!" He responded, "Let us go to the nearby villages that I may preach there also. For this purpose I have come." Not only did he preach throughout Galilee, but he has visited you and me. He is preaching to us at this very moment through the word his Church has made available to us. Everyone matters to him. No one has a fever that he doesn't know about.

Everyone is looking for him—even if they don't know it.

Friday of the First Week
of Ordinary Time • Mark 2:1–12

When Jesus returned to Capernaum, so many people gathered together to hear him preach that there wasn't room for one more person. When some men came, carrying a paralytic, they had to let him down from the roof. When Jesus saw their faith, he said, "Child, your sins are forgiven." When some scribes became uncomfortable with the prospect of Jesus forgiving sins, Jesus said, "Why are you thinking such things in your hearts? Which is easier to say to the paralytic, 'Your sins are forgiven' or to say 'Rise, pick up your mat and walk?' But that you, rise, pick up your mat and go home." Which do you suppose was his greater act of mercy? Well, physically, the man eventually died. But to this day those sins of his are still forgiven!

Saturday of the First Week
of Ordinary Time • Mark 2:13–17

As Jesus walked along the lakeshore with crowds of people coming to him, he noticed Levi, the son of Alphaeus, at his tax collector's post and said to him, "Follow me!" Levi got up and followed him. Later, at Levi's house, some Pharisees asked the disciples of Jesus why he would eat with tax collectors and offenders of the law. Jesus overheard and answered, "Those who are well do not need a physician, but the sick do. I did not come to call the righteous but sinners."

Jesus doesn't seek political correctness or public signs of achievement—still less wealth and power. He doesn't even seek those skilled in the ins and outs of ecclesiastical politics. He seeks the humble wherever they are—those who simply know that they can't make it without him.

Second Sunday of Ordinary Time • Year B
John 1:35–42

As Jesus walked by, John the Baptist saw him and said to his disciples, "Look! There is the Lamb of God!" When Jesus noticed that they were following him, he asked them what they were looking for. They asked him where he was staying. He told them to come and see. They spent most of the day with him. One of them, Andrew, left to get his brother and brought him to the group. When Jesus saw him, he said, "You are Simon, son of John; your name shall be Cephas," which means Peter.

Only John's Gospel gives us this in such detail. This is the context in which Andrew and Peter and Jesus first met. What is the context in which you became friends with the Lord? Was it your family as you grew up? Was it some sort of setback that you experienced? Was it Catholic radio, or perhaps a friend, or your spouse? However it happened, he has plans for you, just as he had for them—and I can assure it has to do with his cross and Resurrection.

Monday of the Second Week
of Ordinary Time • Mark 2:18–22

People asked Jesus why the disciples of John the Baptist and the disciples of the Pharisees fasted while his disciples did not. This was an obvious effort to discredit Jesus and his disciples in the face of the Pharisees' fasting, which they took great pride in—in more ways than one. His response was "Can the wedding guests fast while the bridegroom is with them? . . . But the days will come when the bridegroom will be taken away from them, and then they will fast on that day." The time had to be appropriate. He was concerned that fasting be done as an expression of real repentance and not simply as a display of righteousness, for show, as in the case of the Pharisees. It was truth that he was about.

What inappropriate choices do we make under cover of acceptable or even praiseworthy show? It is the truth that we must be about as well.

Tuesday of the Second Week
of Ordinary Time • Mark 2:23–28

As Jesus was passing through a field of grain on the Sabbath, his disciples began to make a path while picking the heads of grain. The Pharisees immediately accused them of violating the Sabbath. They saw the plucking as manual labor. Actually, they had lost sight of the fundamental purpose of the Sabbath law. Such observance is subordinate to the needs of men, who were not created merely to observe the Sabbath.

We see the same narrowness today in those who set themselves up as authorities and judge the validity of the Church's teachings regarding private revelations, the Second Vatican Council, and anything else they disagree with. But in reality they are setting themselves up against God! Why is it that they never question their own authority? It is only through humility that we hear the truth.

Thursday of the Second Week
of Ordinary Time • Mark 3:7–12

Jesus withdrew to the sea. A large crowd had followed him from Galilee and Judea. He told his disciples to have a boat ready for him so they wouldn't crush him. While the scribes and Pharisees closed their minds and hearts to him, the common people who were hurting recognized that he was no mere popular preacher. He had power that could heal.

When I sit at the computer each day to answer questions on our "Ask an Apologist" forum, I first answer questions from people who seem to be hurting. These are the people our Lord spent himself on the most. They are always the ones most open to him. Actually, at times, we are all such people. We all experience pain at one time or another. What great value our pain has for us! Pain helps us recognize our need for God.

Friday of the Second Week
of Ordinary Time • Mark 3:13–19

Jesus went up the mountain and appointed the Twelve, whom he also named apostles, that they might be with him and that he might send them forth to preach and to have authority to drive out demons. They were to be the duly accredited witnesses who would proclaim the message of salvation after the Lord's death—hence the solemnity attached to their calling. Luke mentions that Jesus spent the previous night in prayer.

Mark stresses that the choices came directly from Jesus. Twelve is the number of the tribes of Israel. They were to be the rulers of the new spiritual Israel, the Church that Jesus was about to establish. Significantly, while the names vary in order in the various lists of apostles given, Judas, the betrayer, is always the last and Peter, the rock, is always the first. For those with eyes to see, the apostolicity of the Catholic Church resides so clearly in Scripture.

Saturday of the Second Week
of Ordinary Time • Mark 3:20–21

The crowds made it impossible for Jesus and his disciples even to eat. Some who were close to him in the past didn't understand what they had been hearing about him and set out to seize him because they thought he was mad. I'm reminded of St. Bernadette at Lourdes, when Our Lady told her to bathe in the spring and all she could find was some mud, which she rubbed on her hands and face. Her mother came and took her away as bystanders jeered, thinking her to be mad. But as time passed, the mud became a spring from which the Lord has healed thousands of their infirmities to this very day.

Isaiah 55 says, "For my thoughts are not your thoughts, nor are your ways my ways, says the Lord." And for our consolation, Psalm 103 tells us, "As far as the east is from the west so far he removes our transgressions from us." We could all use more of such divine madness.

Third Sunday of Ordinary Time
Year B • Mark 1:14–20

After John the Baptist's arrest, Jesus began proclaiming God's good news in Galilee, "The reign of God is at hand!" It was here that he began to call fishermen to be his apostles. "Come after me; I will make you fishers of men," he said. Immediately they abandoned their nets and followed him.

Notice who Jesus didn't begin with. He didn't go to the educated or those familiar with religious matters. He went to the unsophisticated, to those who knew that there was much that they didn't know. They were the ones who were likely to be the most open to him. In our time, Pope John Paul did the same thing. He focused on the world's youth because he knew that they would be the most receptive. Initially some thought that he was unrealistic—an old man trying to connect with the young. But the connection was immediate. Today, Pope John Paul remains with us in what we call "the John Paul II generation." It is from them that the future leaders of the Church are coming and already beginning to lead.

Monday of the Third Week
of Ordinary Time • Mark 3:22–30

The scribes accused Jesus of being possessed by Beelzebul. "By the prince of demons, he drives out demons," they said. Jesus easily shows their complete lack of reason. "How can Satan drive out Satan?" he asked.

Jesus then clearly stated that whoever blasphemes against the Holy Spirit will never have forgiveness. By attributing the merciful actions of Jesus to those of Satan, the scribes were actually guilty of diabolical malice themselves. Such statements were clearly an example of willful malice and blindness to the light. As long as they persisted in that mentality, pardon was impossible—not because of a limitation of God's mercy but because of their refusal to respond to the promptings of grace.

There is no reason to fear committing such an unpardonable sin—as long as we don't want to. Our choices are entirely ours. So long as we choose to submit to the Lord, we will always know his mercy—always!

Tuesday of the Third Week
of Ordinary Time • Mark 3:31–35

When Mary, the Mother of Jesus, and other relatives were waiting for Jesus outside, they sent word to him inside. Jesus was told that they were asking for him.

He responded that whoever does the will of the Father is family to him. This in no way discredits his Mother or his cousins, but it does say much about the effects of grace and the relationship he has chosen to have with us.

We're all familiar with those well-meaning persons who elevate their pets to the level of human beings—often to the detriment of the pets when they give them inappropriate food. Animals are animals, and we don't have the power to raise them to the human level in any real way. But God does have the power to raise us to his divine level. Here he makes this quite clear. It remains for us to accept his invitation by always trying to do the will of the Father.

Feast of the Conversion of St. Paul

Wednesday of the Third Week
of Ordinary Time • Mark 16:15–18

Jesus appeared to the Eleven and said, "Go into the whole world and proclaim the Gospel to every creature." Today we celebrate the conversion of St. Paul, a seemingly unlikely candidate for accepting the Gospel—especially after having persecuted so many, including the deacon, St. Stephen. But the Lord had plans for him. From his conversion to his death, all that St. Paul was able to accomplish was the result of the grace God gave him and his willingness to cooperate with it.

This is really no different from you and me. The same Lord has given us the gift to believe—when left on our own we easily could have been unbelievers. And there is no limit to what he can accomplish in the likes of us if he has a mind to—and if we are willing to cooperate. Of course it means carrying the cross as St. Paul did. But what better way is there to respond to the blood Jesus so willingly shed for us?

Thursday of the Third Week
of Ordinary Time • Mark 4:21–25

Jesus asked, "Is a lamp brought in to be placed under a bushel basket or under a bed, and not to be placed on a lamp stand? For there is nothing hidden except to be made visible; nothing is secret except to come to light."

There's no doubt about it—the truth has a way of eventually being made known. This shouldn't be surprising: Truth is the only thing that lasts because it simply reflects what is. The lie reflects nothing. Sooner or later the lie will be seen for what it is—or, better, for what it is not.

The lie causes us to be divided within ourselves. We are then plagued with the need to cover it with ongoing lies. To be humble is to be open to the truth—even if it consists of the worst that can be said of us. Never to fear the truth is to be truly free. It is also to belong completely to him.

Friday of the Third Week
of Ordinary Time • Mark 4:26–34

Jesus said to the crowds, "This is how it is with the Kingdom of God; it is as if a man were to scatter seed on the land and would sleep and rise night and day and the seed would sprout and grow, how, he does not know. Of its own accord the land yields the fruit, first the blade, then the ear, then the full grain in the ear. And when the grain is ripe, he wields the sickle at once for the harvest has come."

The kingdom of God also develops gradually and no less surely until it reaches consummation. Our ordinary life in Christ is a day-to-day thing. It develops in a seemingly ordinary way. Usually, for most of us there are no great revelations or fireworks. But through the daily ups and downs of human life, if we are faithful, harvest time eventually comes and we finally meet the love of our lives and enter eternity with him.

Saturday of the Third Week
of Ordinary Time • Matthew 4:35–41

Jesus and the disciples were on a boat at night when a violent squall came up and the boat began to fill with water. By this time Jesus was asleep on a cushion in the stern. When they woke him for fear of perishing, he quieted the storm to a peaceful calm. Then he asked why they were so terrified. "Do you not yet have faith?"

What about our fears? Faith can calm fear quite effectively. But first we must acknowledge the fear and then identify it. This can be particularly difficult for men, since our culture tends to see being afraid as unmanly. It isn't, of course. It is only in the face of fear that men can act with courage. The one thing that we all fear the most is not having any value. When the disciples woke Jesus, he showed them that he considered them worth protecting. To have faith in him is to know this about ourselves as well.

Fourth Sunday of Ordinary Time
Year B • Mark 1:21–28

Jesus began to teach in the synagogue in Capernaum where he'd freed a man with an unclean spirit. The people were spellbound by the authority of his preaching and by his authority over spirits.

Authority comes from the word *author*, which is *autor* in Latin and means enlarger, or one who makes or originates something. Authority means the power or right to give commands or enforce obedience. No one has more authority over something than the one who is its author. This became very clear to the people who heard and saw Jesus. He spoke with authority because, being the author along with the Father, he was completely sure of himself. Rather early on he gave authority to his apostles over unclean spirits. Later he was to give authority to Peter and his successors. The pope speaks with that same authority today. It results in clear and consistent teaching that ultimately originates not from the pope but from the Author.

Monday of the Fourth Week
of Ordinary Time • Mark 5:1–20

Jesus encountered a man who had been possessed by a demon. The man prostrated himself before Jesus—even though until that time he harassed anyone who came near him. But when Jesus asked the demon's name, it said, "Legion is my name. There are many of us." It immediately became obvious to the evil spirits that Jesus wielded power that was highly superior to theirs. The people of the area became frightened of Jesus and wanted him to leave. However, the man who was freed of the evil spirits wanted to remain with him.

How often are we like those people, fearing the wrong things? Seldom do we fear temptation. But we usually fear the crosses in our lives—which actually have the purpose of helping us come closer to the Lord. We need to recognize the power of his love and our proximity to it.

Wednesday of the Fourth Week
of Ordinary Time • Mark 6:1–6

When Jesus came to his native place and began to teach in the synagogue, the people were at first impressed, but because they knew his origins, they refused to take him seriously. So he did not perform any mighty deeds there, apart from curing a few sick people.

How familiar has he become to us, in the sense that we don't expect much from him? If we've been Catholics all our lives, how much do we take our faith for granted? If we can become numb to the qualities of those with whom we live and can see each day, then what about him, whom we cannot see? We need to see him daily. A good place to start is by reading Scripture—or meditating on a crucifix. St. Thomas Aquinas said that he learned more from looking at the cross than from any book he ever read. When we truly desire to behold him in our lives, we will.

Feast of the Presentation of the Lord

Thursday of the Fourth Week
of Ordinary Time • Luke 2:22–40

When Joseph and Mary took the child Jesus to the temple to present him to the Lord, Simeon, a holy and devout man, took him in his arms and said, "Now, Master, you may let your servant go in peace, according to your word, for my eyes have seen your salvation, which you prepared in the sight of all the peoples: a light for revelation to the Gentiles, and the glory for your people Israel."

He was saying that he was ready to die. Holding his Savior in his arms satisfied every desire he had ever had in life. Not only did his physical eyes see his Redeemer; his eyes of faith saw him. His Redeemer was completely present to him in his life. How would you like to be Simeon and have that same experience? Does it sound out of reach? Try receiving Holy Communion tomorrow.

Friday of the Fourth Week
of Ordinary Time • Mark 6:14–29

King Herod, because of the guilt he felt for having put John the Baptist to death, was concerned that Jesus was really John come back to life. It is amazing how distorted one's view of life can become over the refusal to acknowledge past sins. The real tragedy is that Jesus was the only answer to his plight and was so nearby. Yet Herod was not disposed to to recognize him.

Three years later, when Pilate sent Jesus to Herod on Good Friday, he actually met Jesus and treated him as if he were a fool. Again he failed to recognize the only one who could make him whole.

The question remains: When do *we* fail to recognize him? The answer: Every time we sin mortally.

Saturday of the Fourth Week
of Ordinary Time • Mark 6:30–34

Jesus took the apostles away to a deserted place to rest after ministering to so many people that they hadn't even a chance to eat. When the people learned where they were, they came, seeking further help. Upon seeing them, Jesus was moved with compassion and began to teach them.

Something about him made them realize that they were not enough for themselves, and that he had what they needed. They would not have had a name for it. We call it grace—the same grace that enables us to appreciate who he is. But sometimes we forget how much we need him. We get so caught up in ourselves that we begin to act as if we don't need him at all. If we are fortunate, some difficulty will befall us that we are helpless to alleviate. After feeling sorry for ourselves and complaining, if we are further fortunate, light will dawn on us and we'll realize that he is the only one who can help. His love for us is a patient love.

Fifth Sunday of Ordinary Time
Year B • Mark 1:29–39

Jesus had no sooner entered Simon's house when Simon, Andrew, James, and John informed him that Simon's mother-in-law was ill with a fever. So he went to her, grasped her hand, and she was well. In the evening they brought the ill and possessed to him and he healed them all. Early the next morning he went to a deserted place to pray, but his disciples managed to find him and told him, "Everyone is looking for you!" He responded that they must move on to the other villages to proclaim the good news because that was what he had come to do. Notice how everybody was looking for him because he could heal them of obvious maladies. Yet, according his own words, he was there to proclaim the good news. In order to do this, he used their infirmities to show them that they needed him.

I'm old enough to remember that during World War II the churches were filled. Again after September 11, 2001, the same thing. It is when we are hurting that we make room for him. He loves us too much to leave us on our own.

Monday of the Fifth Week
of Ordinary Time • Mark 6:53–56

As soon as Jesus and his disciples left the boat at Gennesaret, people began to bring the sick to him on mats. Whatever villages he entered, they laid the sick in the marketplaces. They begged that they might only touch the tassel of his cloak. The combination of faith and humility always brought miracles—and it still does.

In a culture of cynicism and arrogance, such virtues are often nowhere to be found—until we hurt. In the aftermath of September 11, 2001, concerns over the separation of church and state and political correctness were not in evidence on the streets of New York City, where religious pictures and vigil lights lined so many sidewalks. For a time, America was humbled and began to walk with the Lord. We've drifted again. It's time for America once again to embrace the cross. As always, it remains our only hope.

Tuesday of the Fifth Week
of Ordinary Time • Mark 7:1–13

Scribes and Pharisees noticed that some of the disciples of Jesus ate their meals with unwashed hands. They found this failure to perform the ritual washing of hands before eating a suitable opportunity to renew their attack on Jesus. But Jesus responded by attacking them for dwelling on the minutiae of the Law while passing over the essential aspects, such as the care of aging parents. "Well did Isaiah prophesy about you hypocrites as it it written: 'This people honors me with their lips, but their hearts are far from me; in vain do they worship me, teaching as doctrines human precepts.'"

Today we see a similar hypocrisy in the talk of women's right to choose to have an abortion or not—while at the same time ignoring the thousands of unborn female children whose very lives are snuffed out as the result of such a choice. In vain does anyone worship who lives such a lie.

Wednesday of the Fifth Week
of Ordinary Time • Mark 7:14–23

Jesus told the crowds, "Hear me, all of you, and understand. Nothing that enters one from the outside can defile a person; but the things that come from within are what defile." He later clarified for the disciples that food does not corrupt a person, but sin does. Evil thoughts, unchastity, theft, murder, adultery, envy, malice, and deceit—these things originate in the human heart and come out of the person. Besides declaring all food to be clean, Jesus also refined and redefined the Law in terms of the Spirit. This paves the way for his future statements regarding the morality not just of one's actions but of one's intentions even before acting.

Centuries later St. Thomas Aquinas was to place all morality within the will. When asked how to become a saint, he answered in the spirit of the new Law: "Will it!"

Thursday of the Fifth Week
of Ordinary Time • Mark 7:24–30

While in the district of Tyre, Jesus tried to enter a house unnoticed. But a Greek woman whose daughter had an unclean spirit begged him to drive the demon out. He responded, "Let the children be fed first. For it is not right to take the food of the children and throw it to the dogs." He was telling her that he came first for the benefit of the believing Jews—and not the Gentiles. But she answered, "Lord, even the dogs under the table eat the children's scraps." Such faith and humility was too much for his sacred heart. "For saying this, you may go," he said. "The demon has gone out of your daughter." This was her God, speaking to her, a Gentile.

This is the same God we pray to—or not—each morning and night. We can all learn from our sister Gentile's faith and humility.

Saturday of the Fifth Week
of Ordinary Time • Mark 8:1–10

Jesus had been speaking to a large crowd and was concerned that they had not eaten for three days. So from seven loaves of bread and a few fish, he miraculously fed them all. He didn't need to make himself credible by working a miracle; the people were obviously taken with him if they had remained there all that time without leaving to eat. He fed them because he loved them. This, of course, was only a sign of what was to come. Eventually, he was going to feed them with himself as an expression of the sacrifice of his own human life for them. Even today, Christians who accept the Eucharist as the miracle that it is recognize that they can't fully wrap their minds around the reality of the love that it expresses. It tells us that God loves us so much that he took on a human nature, sacrificed himself on the cross to redeem us, and enters into our very bodies in the most intimate of unions to motivate us to love him.

Sixth Sunday of Ordinary Time
Year B • Mark 1:40–45

A leper approached Jesus and said, "If you wish, you can make me clean." Jesus replied, "I will do it. Be made clean." Immediately he was healed. Jesus warned him not to tell anyone but to go make the offering that Moses prescribed for such things so he would be considered clean according to the Law of Moses. But he was so overjoyed at his healing that he went about telling everybody. As the result, people began inundating Jesus with requests for healing, and he had to stay in deserted places.

It wasn't that he didn't want to heal people, but his purpose in coming to earth was not primarily to heal people of their physical illnesses but to heal them of their spiritual illnesses. Physical illness was not a threat to their salvation, but sin was! This is a hard one for us because ordinarily we can't see what a betrayal of the Lord one mortal sin is. It can be far more terminal than cancer or a heart attack. Heaven and hell begin right here on earth, depending on whether we really love the Lord or not.

Monday of the Sixth Week
of Ordinary Time • Mark 8:11–13

The Pharisees began to argue with Jesus, seeking a sign from heaven to test him. He sighed from the depth of his spirit and said, "Why does this generation seek a sign? Amen, I say to you, no sign will be given to this generation." Then he left, got into a boat, and went off to the other shore. He knew their insincerity and that he had become their enemy because he acted independently of them and opposed much of their behavior.

Even today it is quite possible to appear to subscribe to the teachings of one's religion, while all the while seeking to disregard those teachings in favor of one's own agenda. The Lord is just as aware of such dishonesty today as he was of that of the Pharisees. Most often such individuals are not as aware. They refuse to look as themselves honestly. The key for us not to fall into such self-deception is to humbly submit to him in the teaching authority of the Church.

Wednesday of the Sixth Week
of Ordinary Time • Mark 8:22–26

People brought a blind man to Jesus and begged him to touch him. Jesus took the blind man by the hand to a private place, performed a ritual, as he had recently done with a deaf man, and healed him. He put spittle on the man's eyes and then asked what he could see. At first the man's sight was problematic. So Jesus laid his hands on him a second time and the man saw clearly. Jesus' concern was not with making a public statement but with ministering to one of his own in need. He also seemed to deliberately heal the man slowly, in a step-by-step process, thereby showing his disciples that spiritual growth is a process as well.

This is how he ministers to us. Our spiritual journey is a process—not a once-and-for-all experience. We grow by steps. We slip back, we repent, we are forgiven, and we proceed. It's a kind of breathing in and out—with the breath of the Holy Spirit.

Thursday of the Sixth Week
of Ordinary Time • Mark 8:27–33

As Jesus walked with his disciples, he asked, "Who do people say that I am?" They answered, "John the Baptist, others Elijah, still others one of the prophets" "But you," he said, "who do you say that I am?" Peter responded, "You are the Christ." Jesus then warned him not to tell anyone about this. Then he explained that he would have to suffer greatly, be killed, and in three days rise. He was definitely not the kind of Messiah people wanted and expected. They wanted a Messiah who would triumph over their enemies. Instead, they were getting a suffering servant Messiah who was to conquer by sacrificial love.

So often we don't understand the directions our lives take because we too expect him to be a Messiah who enables us to vanquish all opposition. Instead, we find a Messiah who invites us to love through sacrifice. Such love can transform us into the loving persons he created us to be.

Friday of the Sixth Week
of Ordinary Time • Mark 8:34–9:1

Jesus said, "Whoever wishes to come after me, must deny himself, take up his cross and follow me. For whoever wishes to save his life will lose it, but whoever loses his life for my sake and that of the Gospel will save it."

Where do we hear anything about taking up our crosses or denying ourselves but in the Catholic Church? This is a passage that many like to skip. They prefer the ones that speak of simply proclaiming one's faith in the Person of Jesus and that's that—they're saved. So we do the sinning, he does the suffering—and we go scot-free. Those who have been the closest to him have suffered the most. All his apostles were martyred except John, who stood at the foot of his cross with his Mother—the most painful place for those who loved him. What about you? Do you prefer an easy way out, or do you think that his sacrificial love for you deserves a love that is more than just words?

Saturday of the Sixth Week
of Ordinary Time • Mark 9:2–13

Jesus took Peter, James, and John up a high mountain, where he was transfigured before them. His clothes became a very bright white and Elijah and Moses appeared and conversed with him. The apostles were so terrified that their speech didn't make any sense. Then the Father spoke from a cloud above them, saying, "This is my beloved Son. Listen to him." Suddenly it was all over and they were alone with Jesus, who ordered them to keep silence about it "until the Son of Man had risen from the dead." And this they didn't understand at all.

When one considers all they heard and saw, it is obvious that there was so much they just didn't get. This is really comforting for us to ponder. We miss a lot, too, but we haven't had the advantage of the private instruction that Jesus gave them, though we do have the advantage of hindsight. His love and patience with them tells us a lot about his attitude toward us.

Seventh Sunday of Ordinary Time
Year B • Mark 2:1–12

Word got around that Jesus was back in Capernaum. People had gathered in such great numbers that they blocked the door where he was speaking. At one point, four men arrived, carrying a paralyzed man for healing. Because of the number of people, they let the man down on a pallet through an opening they made in the roof. The man ended up at the feet of Jesus. Moved by their faith, Jesus said to the man, "My son, your sins are forgiven." Of course, the scribes and Pharisees present were upset because they considered such talk to be blasphemy. Only God can forgive sins. Jesus then said, "Why do you harbor such thoughts? Which is easier to say to the paralytic, 'Your sins are forgiven,' or to say, 'Stand up! Pick up your mat and go home.'" The man stood up and walked outside in full view of everyone.

Of course, the greater gift was the forgiveness of sins. Yet we so easily put off going to confession—and we don't even need to make a hole in the roof!

Tuesday of the Seventh Week
of Ordinary Time • Mark 9:30–37

Jesus told his disciples that he would be handed over to men who would kill him and in three days he would rise. However, they did not understand what he was saying and were afraid to question him. A little later, he asked them what they had been discussing along the way. But they remained silent because they had been arguing about who was the greatest. They were closed to what he had been saying because it did not sound pleasant. It could even mean some sort of loss for them. So they simply shut him out.

He knew exactly where they were and did not chastise them. He explained that anyone who wishes to be first must be willing to be the last and the servant of all. By his patience he eventually brought them around. Such was his love for them. Such is his love for the likes of you and me as well. It is his patient love for us that will bring us home.

Ash Wednesday • Lent
Matthew 6:1–6, 16–18

Jesus warned his disciples that their penitential acts must be just that and not a means to draw attention and praise to themselves as hypocrites do. Their love for God had to be the real thing. God deserves nothing less.

But this was not to say that they shouldn't give good example. The distinction between the two was in their intention. If it was God they were focused on, this would inevitably show.

So with us. Today we wear ashes on our forehead—not to draw attention to ourselves, but to bear witness to the fact that we all will eventually die and that we need to acknowledge to God all that we owe him before that day comes. "Remember, man, you are dust and to dust you shall return" (Gn 3:19).

Thursday after Ash Wednesday
Luke 9:22–25

After telling his disciples that he must suffer, be put to death, and then rise, Jesus said, "If anyone wishes to come after me, he must deny himself and take up his cross daily and follow me." Nowhere in our lives will we ever find anyone else saying anything like this.

When people want our allegiance, whether it's to vote for them or buy what they are selling or just give them attention, they appeal to our desire for pleasure or money or some easily identified good. Jesus undercut all this. What profit is there for one to gain the whole world yet lose or forfeit his self, he says. To be his disciple is to carry the cross, but it is also to be entirely his. What could be better than that? A-b-s-o-l-u-t-e-l-y nothing!

Friday after Ash Wednesday
Matthew 9:14–15

The disciples of John the Baptist asked Jesus why his disciples did not fast while they and the Pharisees did. Jesus responded that the wedding guests could not mourn while the bridegroom was still with them, but the day would come when he would be taken away—and then they would fast. Jesus obviously associates wedding festivities with joy and not sorrow, as in the case of fasting.

The time did come for his disciples to fast, and it continues to this day. We fast in reparation for our infidelity toward him—considering all that he endured for us! Fasting is a way of asserting our conviction that gives credibility to our words before others—but most importantly to ourselves. After all, fasting is a form of sacrifice—and sacrifice is the measure of love.

Saturday after Ash Wednesday
Luke 5:27–32

Jesus said to a tax collector named Levi, "Follow me," and the man stood up, left everything, and became his disciple. Later, Levi gave a great reception for Jesus at his house. Many of the guests were tax collectors. Observant Jews saw them as nonobservant as well as collaborators with the Romans, under whom the Jews were subject in their own country. So the Pharisees asked Jesus' disciples why they ate and drank with such people. Jesus overheard them and responded that only the sick need doctors. "I have not come to invite the self-righteous to a change of heart, but sinners," he said.

When Levi responded by following Jesus, he left everything, so that Jesus became his most prized possession. Is this also true of us, who consider ourselves his followers? Certainly, we who observe this Saturday in Lent fit right in with Levi and his friends because we acknowledge that we are sinners in desperate need of a divine Doctor.

First Sunday of Lent • Year B
Mark 1:12–15

The Spirit sent Jesus out to the desert for forty days to be tempted. Satan wanted to discover whether he was the Messiah and, if possible, to lead him from the path of suffering to follow him. But Satan, with his keen angelic intellect, was a fool. Jesus allowed himself to be tempted for the sake of assisting us sinners by sharing in our human journey in all things but sin. Of course, he remained faithful to his Father throughout his ordeal and returned from the desert to begin his public life.

Often when we are about to take on a sizeable responsibility or engage in an important task, we will have some difficulty, like catching a cold or a bout with temptation or immature behavior that we thought we had overcome in the past. This is usually the Lord reminding us to stay focused on him and on how much we need him—a divine reality check, if you will.

First Monday of Lent • Matthew 25:31–46

Jesus told his disciples that when he comes in his glory, he will sit on his throne with all the nations assembled before him. He will then separate them as a shepherd separates the sheep from the goats. Those on his right will inherit the kingdom prepared from the foundation of the world. He will explain, "For I was hungry and you gave me food, I was thirsty and you gave me drink, a stranger and you welcomed me, naked and you clothed me, ill and you cared for me, in prison and you visited me . . . whatever you did for one of the least of my brothers, you did for me."

Who are the least of his brothers in our lives—someone we don't like or don't care to know, the unborn children we have done nothing to protect? There are, no doubt, others. Whose are the faces of Christ that we fail to recognize?

First Tuesday of Lent • Matthew 6:7–15

Jesus said, "In praying, do not babble like the pagans who think they will be heard because of their many words. Do not be like them. Your Father knows what you need before you ask him." Certainly, the last thing we do when we pray is inform God of what he doesn't know. We may inform ourselves, but not him. We pray first of all to acknowledge him and his generosity to us. This is what *latria* or worship or adoration is. We can properly address no other in this way. When we rejoice over such acknowledgment, we call it praise, as in the Gloria and Holy, Holy, Holy at Mass. When we ask pardon, we pray for contrition as in the Act of Contrition, and when we ask for what we need, as in the Prayer of the Faithful, our prayer is one of petition.

All these forms of prayer can be found in the one prayer our Blessed Lord taught us: the Our Father or the Lord's Prayer. Amen!

First Wednesday of Lent • Luke 11:29–32

Jesus said to the people as they gathered before him, "This generation is an evil generation; it seeks a sign, but no sign will be given it, except the sign of Jonah. Just as Jonah was a sign to the Ninevites, so will the Son of Man be to this generation." Jonah went through the streets shouting, "Forty days more and Nineveh will be overthrown." The king proclaimed a fast and all the people and animals fasted with sackcloth and ashes, and God had mercy on them.

What is the sign for our generation? Could it be the same sign? Lent is roughly forty days. And certainly, a generation that kills so many of the young it has just conceived is evil enough. Penance and prayer, self-denial, and true contrition—such must be our response. Nothing else will do.

First Thursday of Lent • Matthew 7:7–12

When someone asked on our "Ask an Apologist" forum if it is a sin to pray for oneself, I answered that it is far from a sin and is actually a command. In Matthew 7:7 Jesus said to his disciples, "Ask and it will be given to you; seek and you will find; knock and the door will be opened to you." He then asked who of us would give a stone to one's son when he asked for bread or a snake when he asked for a fish. If we who are sinful know how to give gifts to our children, how much more does God who is our heavenly Father!

We find ourselves feeling guilty for praying for ourselves because it still hasn't sunken in that he really loves us. If hanging three hours on the cross hasn't convinced us, we need to spend more time looking at a crucifix. In that personal effort to look and behold his suffering, we will see that such love is aimed directly and personally at us.

First Friday of Lent • Matthew 5:20–26

Jesus told his disciples, "I tell you, unless your righteousness surpasses that of the scribes and Pharisees, you will not enter the Kingdom of heaven." He then proceeded to fine-tune the requirements of the Old Law regarding anger toward one's brother, bringing a gift to the altar without being reconciled with one's brother, and holding a grudge with one's opponent.

He was not concerned with outward observance only, as the scribes and Pharisees were, but with one's inner disposition. Heaven demanded more than the lip service they prided themselves on. This seemed to put Jesus at odds with them more than anything else. He showed great patience with failures resulting from human weakness, which humble us. But he roundly condemned willful hypocrisy every time because it is always accompanied by prideful arrogance.

We do well to remember that it is only his mercy that will ever justify us.

First Saturday of Lent • Matthew 5:43–48

Jesus told his disciples to love their enemies and to pray for their persecutors. This will prove that they are sons of their heavenly Father who sustains the bad as well as the good. Have you ever thought what life would be like if Jesus didn't love his enemies and persecutors? There would be little hope for them. There would be no conversions. There would be no St. Paul, no St. Mary Magdalene, no St. Peter—actually, we'd all be a bunch of enemies. But then if he didn't love us, we wouldn't even exist.

For love to be love, it has to be unselfish and centered on the good of others and not just the pleasure we receive from them. The Lord's way is the only one that really works. We are wired for it. All the totalitarians in history, all the cruel dictators never achieved the happiness they sought because they were focused on themselves. Somehow they got their wires crossed. We are wired for sacrificial love—period!

Second Sunday of Lent • Year B
Mark 9:2–10

Jesus took Peter, James, and John up a high mountain, where he was transfigured before them. His clothes became a very bright white. Elijah and Moses then appeared and were in conversation with Jesus. Peter began to talk about erecting three booths for them and was interrupted by the voice of the Father, speaking from a cloud above them. "This is my Son, my beloved. Listen to him." Suddenly, all was as it had been. As they descended the mountain, Jesus told them not to mention the incident to anyone until the Son of Man had risen from the dead. They complied, but they wondered what "rising from the dead" might mean.

From hindsight we know what was happening, but they didn't have a clue. Nevertheless, it is only because they finally understood that we know about it at all. Obviously, Jesus didn't mean for them to understand at the time. This event was to help them understand later. His timing was flawless. It still is. We usually want to know everything yesterday. But he knows exactly what we need when we need it. It remains for us to love him by trusting him.

Second Monday of Lent • Luke 6:36–38

Jesus said to his disciples, "Be merciful, just as your Father is merciful. . . . Stop judging and you will not be judged. Stop condemning and you will not be condemned. Forgive and you will be forgiven." He wanted them to meet persecution with a superhuman charity that demands the absolute surrender of the self to God's purposes. He cautioned them not to judge themselves better than others and that correction must always begin with themselves.

But, he was not telling them to stop using their intellects in the cause of distinguishing right from wrong! He told them to imitate their heavenly Father's mercy, after all. As we all know, the Father's mercy often expresses itself by correcting and holding people accountable! He shows us that love must always be our motivation.

Second Tuesday of Lent
Matthew 23:1–12

Jesus warned his disciples to observe all that the scribes and Pharisees told them to do but not to follow their example. He acknowledged their authority but took great exception to their behavior, referring to their self-absorption and penchant for places and terms of honor. So he warned about seeking titles of "teacher" or "father." He by no means was suggesting that they stop using such titles for those to whom such titles belonged. Scripture shows us that in themselves such titles have their place. St. Paul called himself the father of those he shepherded.

In this context, Jesus was warning against pride and of being on guard against self-seeking. Such warnings are still appropriate. St. Catherine of Siena was to one day tell the Lord, "My me is You," so centered was she on him. This is what he deserves from all of us.

Second Wednesday of Lent
Matthew 20:17–28

Jesus took the Twelve with him to Jerusalem. On the way he spoke of his Passion. Not long after, the mother of James and John asked that her sons sit one at his left and the other at his right in his kingdom. His reaction was to tell her that she didn't know what she was asking. Besides, being his follower meant seeking the good of others over oneself. He came to serve, not to be served.

Can you imagine what would happen to Madison Avenue if people began operating this way? At first, it might seem that the country would go bankrupt, but actually everyone would benefit because each person would be looking out for his neighbor. The whole advertising industry would have to reverse itself and appeal to everyone's generosity.

This is what God has in mind for you and me. It's what we were designed for.

Second Thursday of Lent
Luke 16:19–31

Jesus told the Pharisees about a rich man who lived quite well and a poor man named Lazarus who lay at his door covered with sores. When they both died, the rich man cried out to Abraham from the netherworld where he was in torment. He asked Lazarus, who rested at the bosom of Abraham, if he could dip his hand in water and cool his tongue, which was in torment from the flames. He was told that this was not possible.

Jesus reverses the traditional notion that wealth and riches are a sign of God's favor. The ultimate goal for his followers is not prosperity, but of depriving oneself of everything for the kingdom of God! There have been Christians (and still are) who have somehow managed to overlook this passage, but the Catholic Church has always upheld it. This is the main reason that it can be such a thorn in the side of cultures like ours.

Second Saturday of Lent
Luke 15:1–3, 11–32

As the scribes and Pharisees griped that Jesus associated with tax collectors and sinners, he told them the parable of the prodigal son. This son asked for his inheritance and then went off and squandered it until he was destitute. Coming to his senses, he returned home to ask his father to treat him as one of his hired hands. But when the father saw him at a distance, he ran to welcome him with open arms and held a great feast for him. When an older son learned of the celebration, he was angered and refused to join in—at which his father explained that his brother had been dead and was now alive. They needed to rejoice that he had come back. Jesus was showing the Pharisees how he looked at the sinners they were rebuffing. Unfortunately, they were in denial that they qualified as such sinners. He would forgive them and there would be reason to rejoice if only they would come to their senses as well. As for us, are we in denial—or do we daily submit to his love?

Third Sunday of Lent • Year B
John 2:13–25

When Jesus entered the temple precincts, he found people engaging in commerce, selling oxen, sheep, and doves. He took a whip of cords and drove them all out, knocking over tables and spilling coins in all directions. "Stop turning my Father's house into a market place." When asked by what authority he did this, he answered, "Destroy this temple and in three days I will raise it up." Of course, no one understood what he was talking about, but after Easter Sunday his disciples remembered and understood.

Even though we may not be able to understand our current challenges, we will see how perfect his will for us always is.

Third Monday of Lent • Luke 4:24–30

Jesus told the people in the synagogue of his hometown of Nazareth, "Amen, I say to you, no prophet is accepted in his own native place." He then used examples of God's favor being shown most frequently to outsiders. The people there were filled with fury and led him to the brow of a hill to hurl him down, but he passed through their midst and went away.

We can learn a lot about a person simply by knowing what upsets him the most. Usually it's whatever we cherish and fear losing—our family, our talents, our control, our youth, our appearance, our status and reputation, all that we still want to accomplish. What about losing our desire to want to please him more than anything—how concerned are we about losing that? If that is our greatest concern, then we don't have to worry about being threatened.

Third Tuesday of Lent • Matthew 18:21–35

Peter asked Jesus, "Lord, if my brother sins against me, how often must I forgive him; as many as seven times?" Jesus answered, "I say to you, not seven times, but seventy-seven times." He then went on to tell him a story of a servant who was unwilling to offer to one who was indebted to him the same mercy he himself had just received.

This matter touches us far more directly than we might like to think. Whom do you refuse to forgive? Or better, whom do you resent? Or better, who is it that really gets under your skin? Bull's-eye! That's who it is, all right. Chances are that person is not asking to be forgiven. But are you willing to forgive such persons should they ask? Better to give thanks for their presence in your life. Gratitude humbles us, removes resentment, and heals us on all sides.

God likes our gratitude, and he *always* deserves it.

Third Wednesday of Lent • Matthew 5:17–19

Jesus said to his disciples, "Do not think that I have come to abolish the law and the prophets. I have come not to abolish but to fulfill." It is in the fulfilling of the law and prophets that he challenges all who hear him. He does not intend to fulfill the law by beginning with outward observance, as his fellow Jews were accustomed to expect. From this point forward, fulfillment of the law had to come from inside the person. Mere outward observance would not be sufficient in itself. It would have to reflect an inner disposition. So often he charged the scribes and Pharisees with appearing blameless on the outside but being full of corruption and deceit inside.

The kingdom of God demands much more. It demands purity of heart. "Blessed are the pure of heart," Jesus was to say, "for they shall see God." To have a pure heart is to prefer nothing to him.

Third Thursday of Lent • Luke 11:14–23

When Jesus has cast out a demon from a mute man, some in the crowd said that it was by the power of Beelzebul, the prince of demons, that he had cast it out. Jesus responded that Satan cannot drive himself out. Then he warned them, "But if it is by the finger of God that I drive out demons, then the kingdom of God has come upon you." If they had so sided against Jesus when he cast out a devil, this in itself was a sign that they had taken sides with Satan!

The kingdom of God had indeed come upon them and found them wanting. How important is the kingdom of God to us? Is it even on our radar? Practically speaking, the kingdom of God is his agenda for us, as is made known through the teaching authority of his Church. How willing are we to drop everything for him and his kingdom?

Third Friday of Lent • Mark 12:28b–34

When a scribe asked Jesus for the first of all commandments, he answered, "Hear, O Israel! The Lord our God is Lord alone! You shall love the Lord your God with all your heart, will all your soul, with all you mind and with all your strength. The second is this: You shall love your neighbor as yourself." Jesus was emphasizing the superiority of the inner spiritual and moral life over exterior observance. When the scribe understood and agreed with him in this, Jesus said to him, "You are not far from the Kingdom of God."

So with us! Take liturgy, for example: Many are the skirmishes over liturgical observance and abuse these days. No matter how legitimate one's concerns may be, one's behavior must remain charitable. When charity leaves, nothing of value remains.

Third Saturday of Lent • Luke 18:9–14

Jesus told of two men who went to the temple to pray. One of them, a Pharisee, prayed, "I give you thanks, O God, that I am not like the rest of men—grasping, crooked, adulterous—or even like this tax collector. I fast twice a week, I pay tithes on all I possess." The tax collector, keeping his distance and eyes cast down, just kept beating his breast and saying, "O God, be merciful to me, a sinner." Only the last man went home justified. Jesus concluded by saying, "For everyone who exalts himself shall be humbled while he who humbles himself shall be exalted."

The first man didn't realize how much he needed God's mercy because he was so focused on himself. We seldom realize how ego-centered we are when we are ego-centered. It is usually only when we are laid low by illness or some other apparent tragedy that we are brought back to reality. We all need to focus on the second man, because he is truly us.

Fourth Sunday of Lent • Year B
John 3:14–21

Jesus spoke of the image of a serpent that Moses held up in the desert. The people had complained to Moses about their life in the desert and cynically longed for the days of their slavery under the Egyptians. So God punished them by sending serpents that bit them and caused many to die. The people then repented and God had Moses fashion a seraph serpent to hold up to the people. Anyone who had been bitten had only to look at the serpent icon on the pole and he was healed. Jesus predicted that he must also be held up so that anyone who would look to him with faith might be given eternal life. God so loved the world, he said, that he gave his only Son, so that whoever believes in him may not die but have eternal life. Jesus used the serpent icon as a symbol for himself.

Solemnity of St. Joseph, Husband of Mary

Fourth Monday of Lent • Luke 2:41–51a

Mary and Joseph experienced that horror that all parents dread: not being able to find their child. The fact that Jesus was already twelve years old didn't prevent them from being beside themselves with worry. They looked for three days before they found Him. "Son, why have you done this to us? Your father and I have been looking for you with great anxiety," Mary said. Jesus responded: "Did you not know that I must be in my Father's house?" The Gospel says that they did not understand his words.

This could well have been the first time Joseph heard him speak of a Father other than himself. His was the unique duty of being a role model for God. It was from Joseph that Jesus in his human nature learned to be a man. No wonder he a father figure for us, too, and the patron of the universal Church. We honor him today.

Fourth Tuesday of Lent • John 5:1–3a, 5–16

A man who had been ill for thirty-eight years lay near a pool of healing called Bethesda. When Jesus saw him, he asked him if he wanted to be well. The man answered that he wasn't able to get down to the pool. So "Jesus said to him, 'Rise, take up your mat, and walk,'" and he was immediately healed and took up his mat and walked.

Later, when the man had learned the identity of Jesus, he was able to give this information to the Jews who wanted to know who it was who had healed him and had him carry his mat on the Sabbath. Their concern for keeping the letter of the Law overshadowed the wonder of the manifestation of God's power before them. Personal agendas can blind people like that—as our sins show us. Today we know the wonder of his gift of life within us as we hear the beating of our hearts. May such wonder not be lost on us in the face of *our* agendas.

Fourth Wednesday of Lent • John 5:17–30

Jesus responded to the Jewish leaders by saying, "My Father is at work until now, so I am at work." This angered them, because he not only broke the Sabbath, but he called God his own Father, making himself equal to God. But he also said, "I cannot do anything on my own; I judge as I hear, and my judgment is just, because I do not seek my own will but the will of the one who sent me."

Sometimes people ask why Jesus seems so subservient to the Father, since he himself is God. As God he is equal to the Father, but as man he defers to him. Throughout his time on earth, his one concern was for doing the Father's will. This is the way of love, and the Holy Trinity shows us how this is done. Love does not seek its own will. When in our lives have we consciously and deliberately deferred to the Lord's will? We might consider this the next time we pray, "Thy will be done."

Fourth Thursday of Lent • John 5:31–47

Jesus confronted his detractors by referring to the testimony of John the Baptist, who testified on his behalf. Even Moses wrote about him, but they were deaf to whatever Jesus said. How fortunate to believe him and therefore to believe in him. Our faith in him is such a delicate and mysterious thing. And yet it can be such a powerful and unyielding thing. It is grace that strengthens it. No one can earn it and no one deserves it.

At what point did you become aware that you really believe that he is God and that he matters more to you than anything you can think of? Can you remember? Or is it that you can't ever remember not believing to some degree? It's a very personal thing, of course, and it differs from person to person. But it is always the effect of his deliberate intervention. It's never an accident. He has chosen you for himself.

Fourth Friday of Lent • John 7:1–2, 10, 25–30

Jesus went to Judea for the Feast of Tabernacles. Because some people recognized him, he cried out, "You know me and also know where I am from." He went on to acknowledge the One who sent him, whom they did not know. "I know him, because I am from him and he sent me," he said. They tried to arrest him, but no one laid a hand on him because his hour had not yet come. He was in control. Later, the reckless abandon of his executioners made them seem to be in control. But he was in control the whole time. His Passion was his deliberate gesture of divine love for his people. It was real and calculated to demonstrate his infinite love in a way we could grasp to some degree.

His hour came as he willed it. And by it you and I have a future in eternity with him where we will be able to thank him and know his pleasure in us.

Fourth Saturday of Lent • John 7:40–53

The people were divided in their opinions about Jesus. Some thought he was a prophet. Others thought he was the Messiah. But others objected that the Messiah was not to come from Galilee. When the chief priests and Pharisees asked the temple guards why they did not apprehend him, they replied that no one had ever spoken as he did. The priests and Pharisees replied in disgust that no one had ever seen *them* being taken in by him and that only those who knew nothing of the Law and accounted for nothing believed in him. And so their pride and arrogance continued to keep them from the only one their inmost hearts desired.

And the lowly and unwanted followed him and allowed him to come close. It is still that way and will always be that way.

Fifth Sunday of Lent • Year B
John 12:20–33

Some Greeks who had been impressed with the triumphal entry of Jesus into Jerusalem on Palm Sunday asked Philip for an opportunity to speak with Jesus. But Jesus knew that his true triumph would come with his Passion. So he did not meet with them. Instead he publicly stated that unless a grain falls to the ground and dies, it will produce no wheat. But if it dies, it will produce much wheat. "My soul is troubled now, yet what should I say—Father, save me from this hour? But it was for this that I came to this hour, Father, glorify your name!"

Was this a preview of his agony in the garden? Actually he suffered and died many times in his mind before he suffered in his body. His human nature was truly human and he dreaded pain as much as any of us does. But on Good Friday, bleeding and in misery, he loved us.

Solemnity of the Annunciation

Fifth Monday of Lent • Luke 1:26–38

God sent the angel Gabriel to a virgin named Mary, who was betrothed to a man named Joseph of the House of David. "Hail, full of grace," he said. "The Lord is with you." Mary was understandably troubled by such an exalted greeting. He urged her to not be afraid because she had found favor with God. She was to bear a son to be named Jesus who would be called the Son of God. When she asked how this would be accomplished since she was still a virgin, the angel told her that the Holy Spirit would come upon her. Therefore, her offspring would be called the Son of God!

No human being has ever been so honored or exalted by God himself. Nothing the Catholic Church can say or do could possibly add what the Father has already done. She is the Mother of our Savior. We only honor her because we worship him.

Fifth Tuesday of Lent • John 8:21–30

Jesus told the people, "If you do not believe that I AM, you will die in your sins." So they asked him, "Who are you?" They just didn't understand. He said, "When you lift up the Son of Man, then you will realize that I AM, and that I do nothing on my own, but I say only what the Father taught me." The use of "I AM" is a direct reference to his divinity, of course. The Father identified himself to Moses as "I AM." The Gospel says, "Because he spoke in this way, many came to believe in him." So with us, this is no benevolent philosopher that we follow. Nor do we see him as a prophet. It is his divinity that overwhelms us. That God would love us so much that he would suffer and die for us singles Christianity out from all other religions. Such love is impossible to comprehend without the grace of faith.

Fifth Wednesday of Lent • John 8:31–42

Jesus said to those Jews who believed in him, "If you remain in my word, you will truly be my disciples, and you will know the truth, and the truth will set you free." There were also some who were hostile to him and responded that they were descendants of Abraham and had never been enslaved. But he answered, "Amen, amen I say to you, everyone who commits sin is a slave to sin."

How few in our culture recognize this truth. So many rail against the Catholic Church for pointing to the only freedom that is possible. It is so much easier to recognize sin's slavery when one is finally free of it. But when one is deep into sin, the thought of the pain of wrenching free of it keeps us in the realm of the lie, and change seems completely impossible. But conversion *is* possible and is the most liberating experience.

Fifth Thursday of Lent • John 8:51–59

Jesus announced that whoever keeps his word will never see death. The others responded, "Now we are sure that you are possessed." They reminded him that Abraham and the prophets were already dead. "Are you greater than our father Abraham, who died?" Jesus assured them, "Before Abraham came to be, I AM." So they picked up stones to throw at him. To them this was unspeakable blasphemy. Or . . . he was the unthinkable: He *was* God! It was unthinkable for them to consider that God would humble himself and visit them in such a way—let alone suffer and die as he was to do.

For many, such a God is beyond them. To them, God would never do such a thing—because if *they* were God, they wouldn't. But God is not merely a bigger version of us. Through our gift of faith we know that he loves us that much, and on Good Friday he showed us that, in fact.

Fifth Friday of Lent • John 10:31–42

When the people picked up rocks to stone Jesus, he said, "I have shown you many good works from my Father; for which of these are you trying to stone me?" They replied that he was a man and was trying to make himself God. He replied that if he did not perform his Father's works, then they need not believe him. But if he did perform such works, they ought at least to recognize that they were the works of his Father and that there had to be some connection between the Father and himself. Such obvious logic was beyond them. This possibility was far more than they were willing to entertain. They had completely closed their minds to him as well as their hearts.

We can ask ourselves: How open are our minds and hearts to him? What are the ramifications of following him that are too much for us? But remember: He did perform those works, and he proved his love for us with his own blood!

Palm Sunday • Year B • Mark 11:1–10

Jesus sent two disciples to the village to untie a tethered colt there and bring it back. As they neared the gate, they found the colt, just as he had said. When some bystanders asked them about taking the colt, they answered that they were following orders from Jesus. So the people let them take it. They then brought the colt to Jesus and threw their cloaks across its back and he sat on it. Then the people began to spread their cloaks and cut reeds on the road before him. The people in procession began to sing, "Hosannah! Blessed is he who comes in the name of the Lord!"

Jesus took the initiative of preparing for this triumphal entry into Jerusalem, fulfilling the messianic prophecies and approving the people's acclamations. Of course, within the week he would demonstrate how different a Messiah he was from their expectations. Even today there are those who would like to fashion him according to their agendas. But the heavens cannot contain him. He is God, after all, and cannot be confined by the likes of us.

Monday of Holy Week • John 12:1–11

When Jesus had dinner with Martha, Mary, and their brother, Lazarus, Mary took a liter of costly perfumed oil and anointed his feet and dried them with her hair. His disciple, Judas Iscariot, complained that the money spent for the oil could have been better used for the benefit of the poor. But Jesus defended her. He knew well that the day was drawing near when those feet would bear his wounded body and would be pierced by a nail. "Let her keep this for the day of my burial," he said.

While Judas and some of the others groused over such expenditure for aromatics, Mary gave her attention to her Lord, and her humble and expansive gesture draws our attention to him. Is this not why we live our lives and the reason we have lives at all? Mary chose the better part.

Tuesday of Holy Week • John 13:21–33, 36–38

Reclining at table with the Twelve, Jesus expressed deep sorrow. "Amen, amen, I say to you, one of you will betray me." They were at a loss as to whom he meant. The apostle John leaned over and asked who it was. Jesus identified Judas as the betrayer by offering him a morsel of food. After Judas left the room, Jesus said, "Now is the Son of Man glorified, and God is glorified in him." These words make quite clear how different God's ways are from those of the world. God is glorified in Judas's betrayal because through it God, in the Person of Jesus, was to suffer and die on the cross for us. In this he was to reveal his infinite love in a way that surpasses any revelation he had ever made of himself. He is glorified in us to the degree that we love him in response.

Wednesday of Holy Week
Matthew 26:14–25

The chief priests paid Judas Iscariot thirty pieces of silver for handing Jesus over to them, and from that time on he looked for an opportunity to accomplish this. Of course, such overt betrayal does not come about in a vacuum. It always has a context. In another passage we read that Judas had been used to helping himself to the common purse, since he was in charge of the money, so he had been betraying his Lord for quite a while.

So with us, our daily habitual behavior affects the overall direction of our lives. Saints become saints one choice at a time. We only love the Lord to the degree that we are completely faithful to him. There cannot be room for some corner in our lives that we reserve to ourselves apart from him. His goodness demands that we prefer nothing to him.

Holy Thursday • John 13:1–15

At the Last Supper, Jesus washed the feet of his apostles. At that time, roads were polluted with dung from all the animals used for transportation. Since sandals didn't give much protection, their feet were usually very foul. To wash someone's feet was quite an act of humility. This is why Peter was so reluctant to allow Jesus to wash his. But it is also the reason Jesus wanted to. It demonstrated his message so well. It is the message of the Eucharist, which he had just given them.

The next day they were to be overwhelmed by what the Eucharist signifies. They were to witness the sacrifice of his body and blood on the cross. It was to take them a while to accept that nothing about us—not the dirt on our feet nor the filth of our sins—can keep God's love from us.

Holy Saturday • Mark 16:1–8

When the Sabbath was over, just after sunrise, Mary Magdalene, Mary the mother of James and John, and Salome brought perfumed oils to anoint Jesus. They wondered how they would move the stone in front of the burial place, but when they arrived, they found that it was already rolled back. In the tomb, a young man in white calmed their fears, for they were quite shaken by his presence. He told them that Jesus was not there and to go and tell the disciples and Peter. Notice how he singled Peter out because Peter was the leader. He assured them that they would see Jesus in Galilee. They left, trembling at what they had just experienced. Although there is no reason to fear contact with the risen Lord, we do well to recognize that we do more than simply know he is risen when we receive him in the Eucharist. At that moment he fills our very being in a most intimate and personal way.

Easter Sunday • John 20:1–9

Mary Magdalene went to the tomb well before dawn. When she found that the stone had been moved aside, she ran and told Peter and John. So the two went to the tomb and Peter entered first, even though John had been ahead of him. There they noticed the body wrappings. John notes that when he saw these things, he believed.

While Jesus had appointed Peter as leader, he gave John special attention, probably because of his youth. John had shown deference to Peter by waiting and letting him enter first. But he is quick to state that he immediately believed—even though none of them had expected Jesus to rise from the dead. Obviously he was given the grace of faith. Perhaps this was inevitable because of the intimacy he shared with his master. Is this why you and I believe? I'd like to think so.

Monday in the Octave of Easter
Matthew 28:8–15

In the account of Matthew, Mary Magdalene went quickly from the tomb on the word of an angel that the Lord had risen. Fearful and yet overjoyed, she ran to announce the news to the apostles. But on the way, she encountered Jesus. "Do not be afraid," he said. "Go tell my brothers to go to Galilee, and there they will see me."

If you were told that you would see him in Galilee, what obstacles would you overcome in order to see him? What would you be willing to endure just to see him? Just to see his face? This is not hypothetical. No doubt we are not likely to be seeing him in Galilee, but we do have the option of seeing him. So the question is relevant: What are we willing to endure to see him? How high a price are we willing to pay? If no price is too high, we will see him, and we will know him as he knows us!

Tuesday in the Octave of Easter
John 20:11–18

In this account of John, Mary Magdalene was weeping outside the tomb when Jesus himself asked her why she wept. She began to answer, thinking that he was the gardener, when he said, "Mary!" At that, she knew him. This account differs from Matthew's, which we considered yesterday. But though the details differ, the essential element is present. The risen Jesus appeared to Mary Magdalene and she was overjoyed at the news that is as fresh today as it was then.

The eternal moment in which his suffering on Good Friday peaked and he died transcends all time. We are there, and the blood that he shed is a part of our lives. We see it as we draw near to the altar. It courses in our veins as we receive it in the Eucharist. He is risen. He is truly risen!

Wednesday in the Octave of Easter
Luke 24:13–35

Two disciples were walking to a village seven miles from Jerusalem on Easter morning. As they were conversing, Jesus joined them, though they did not recognize him. They were downcast because of his death. Like so many other Jews they were accustomed to focusing only on the pleasant aspects of the Messiah in Scripture. They weren't prepared for a Messiah who would suffer and die. So he explained the Scriptures to them and how it all had to be. They urged him to dine with them, and in the breaking of bread they recognized him.

We also tend to focus on the pleasant aspects of the Gospel, forgetting not only the central place of the cross in the Lord's life, but also its central place in our own. It is only in recognizing the necessity of the cross in our lives that we will recognize him in our lives as well.

Thursday in the Octave of Easter
Luke 24:35–48

The disciples who met Jesus on the road had returned to Jerusalem and were recounting their meeting with him to the apostles when Jesus stood in their midst and said the words, "Peace be with you!" He looked at their terrified faces and said, "Why are you troubled?" He showed them his hands and feet and then asked for something to eat. He ate some fish in front of them and this seemed to calm them. He then opened their minds to Scripture as he had done earlier with the two on the road.

Why such fear? Remember, their world had just come crashing down on them. They were afraid of everything. Their protector was now the source of their fear—until they recognized that this man was truly the Jesus they knew. So with us, the better we know him, the easier it is for us to recognize him when we are afraid.

Friday in the Octave of Easter
John 21:1–14

Simon Peter, Thomas, Nathaniel, James, and John were fishing in the Sea of Tiberius. When they saw Jesus standing on shore, he told them to cast their net over the right side of the boat. They did and were not able to pull the net in because of the great number of fish in it. Immediately they recognized him. He already had roasted some fish and they had breakfast with him. The meal was joy-filled. They knew him and had spent so many hours with him that he had become the center of their existence. Being united with him again filled them with delight.

Do you see any parallels here? To the extent that we center our lives around him, to that degree will we be able to delight in his presence in a union that will never end.

Saturday in the Octave of Easter
Mark 16:9–15

Mark 16:9 simply states, "When Jesus rose from the dead early on the first day of the week, he first appeared to Mary Magdalene." She in turn told his disciples, who refused to believe her. But later, Jesus revealed his Resurrection to two of them as they journeyed. They returned to tell the others but met with the same refusal to believe. Then, as they gathered at table, Jesus revealed himself to them and took them to task for their unbelief.

Why didn't they believe? Probably they were afraid to get their hopes up. We tend to forget just how shocking and bloody the Lord's Passion was. They had become so dependent on him, and to have him killed in such a deliberate and crushing manner devastated them. Does it devastate us? If not, we need to reflect on it until it does.

Divine Mercy Sunday

Second Sunday of Easter • Year B
John 20:19–31

Jesus stood before the apostles. "Peace be with you," he said. "As the Father has sent me, so I send you." Then he breathed on them and said, "Receive the Holy Spirit. If you forgive men's sins, they are forgiven them; if you hold them bound, they are held bound." This is when mere men were given the power to forgive sins. From that time to the present day, he has forgiven his people's sins through the persons of his priests in a personal and intimate way. Significantly, they cannot absolve their own sins but must be absolved by another priest. It is not their forgiveness that they bestow, but his.

Then he called Thomas, who had refused to believe that he had risen. He told him to examine his wounds. The scars on his body spoke of his humanity. The fact that he was alive spoke of his divinity. In response, Thomas fell before him and exclaimed, "My Lord and my God." If we believe, those words are ours as well.

Monday of the Second Week of Easter
John 3:1–8

A Pharisee named Nicodemus came to Jesus in the night. He acknowledged Jesus as a teacher from God because he knew that no one could perform the signs he was performing unless he was from him. This was quite an acknowledgment for a Pharisee to make! Jesus explained to him that unless one is born from above, he cannot enter the kingdom of God. Nicodemus asked how an adult can reenter the womb and be born again. Jesus answered, "Amen, amen, I say to you unless one is born from above, he cannot see the Kingdom of God."

So it is in the waters of baptism that we are born again. He cautions us not to be amazed. Just as the wind blows without our knowing its origin or destination, but only hearing its sound, so how the Spirit births us we don't know. We only see and hear the baptismal water and believe his words.

Tuesday of the Second Week of Easter
John 3:7b–15

Jesus continues to speak of baptism to Nicodemus, who asks how one can be born from above.

"You are the teacher of Israel and you do not understand this?" Jesus asks. "Amen, amen, I say to you, we speak of what we know and we testify to what we have seen, but you people do not accept our testimony. If I tell you about earthly things and you do not believe, how will you believe if I tell you about heavenly things? No one has gone up to heaven except the one who has come down from heaven, the Son of Man." He then says that just as Moses lifted up the bronze serpent to heal those who had been bitten by snakes, so he must be lifted up so that everyone who looks at him with faith may have eternal life. The mystery of baptism is actually the mystery of who he is and why he came—and you and I are a part of that mystery.

Wednesday of the Second Week of Easter
John 3:16–21

Jesus says that God so loved the world that he gave his only-begotten Son so that everyone who believes in him might not perish but have eternal life. He did not send him to condemn, but to save. He is the light who has come into the world. Those whose works are evil prefer the darkness. But those who live in truth come to Jesus, the light, so that their works can be seen.

People who live in the darkness tend to be bitter, negative, and very unhappy and usually blame others for their unhappiness. But those who have put their faith in him have every reason to be hopeful—no matter how difficult their lives may seem. We were created to respond to the truth of his love. The more devoted we are to him, the more we are truly ourselves. He is the light of our lives.

Thursday of the Second Week of Easter
John 3:31–36

John the Baptist states that the one who comes from the earth is earthly and speaks of earthly things. But the one who comes from heaven is above all. Whoever accepts his testimony certifies that God is trustworthy. How we look at life and how we live it depends on whether we find God trustworthy or not. It all comes down to that, doesn't it? When we sin, we determine that we deserve to have our way over God's. We act as if we are more trustworthy. But we don't actually stop and reason the whole thing out. If we did, we would be far less likely to sin.

What he wants from us is our trust—which is another word for faith. To trust him is to value him. To have faith in him is to recognize who he is and that he is everything to us.

APRIL 20, 2012

Friday of the Second Week of Easter
John 6:1–15

When Jesus had crossed the Sea of Galilee, a large crown followed him because they saw the signs he was performing. When he noticed the size of the crowd, he took five barley loaves and two fish and miraculously fed them all—with food left over.

It has been suggested that the people actually had more food than was previously apparent and that the real miracle lay in the fact that they actually shared what they had with each other. There is absolutely no evidence of this in the Gospel. This stance suggests that there is more value in a purely human explanation than in having faith in the Lord's ability to work a miracle. But over and over Jesus said to those he healed, "It is your faith that has saved you." Nowhere do we find him saying, "It is your natural explanation that has saved you." Such lack of faith will never save us. Our only hope lies in our faith in him.

Saturday of the Second Week of Easter
John 6:16–21

The disciples came down to the lake and embarked for Capernaum. After three or four miles of heavy rowing, they saw Jesus walking toward them on the water and became frightened. "It is I. Do not be afraid," he said.

The unknown scares us because it makes us feel vulnerable. We don't know how to protect ourselves and we lose our sense of well-being. The disciples experienced this often with Jesus, but nothing prepared them for the fear they experienced at his death. Ironically, it is his death that gives us the greatest comfort when we delve into what it truly is. By experiencing death, he joined us in ours. For those who love him, death is not something we experience alone. We fear it for the same reason the disciples feared the unknown element in his walking on the water. But when we breathe our last, he will be there. "It is I; do not be afraid."

Third Sunday of Easter • Year B
Luke 24:35–48

As the disciples were recounting their meeting with Jesus on their way to Emmaus, Jesus stood in the midst of them there in the upper room. They all became frightened. "Look at my hands and feet. . . . Touch me, and see that a ghost does not have flesh and bones as I do." he said. To put them further at ease, he asked for something to eat. Then he reminded them of the words he had spoken to them in the past about how all that had been written about him had to be fulfilled, how the Messiah must suffer and rise from the dead on the third day. In his name, penance for the remission of sins was to be preached to all the nations, beginning at Jerusalem. He told them that they were now witnesses to this.

So we learn something of what a glorified body is like. It is substantial and retains its ability to consume food. Jesus retained scars from his Passion as a testimony to it and as proof of who he is. When we finally see him, we will see them.

Monday of the Third Week of Easter
John 6:22–29

After Jesus had fed the five thousand, the next day the crowds got into boats in search of him. When they arrived on the opposite shore, they asked him when he had arrived. He answered that he knew that they were only interested in him because of the loaves he had multiplied. "Do not work for food that perishes," he said, "but for food that endures to eternal life, which the Son of Man will give you."

There is in us mortals a stubborn tendency to limit him to the merely earthly mode. We have seen this recently in the attempt in some circles to interpret his miracle of the loaves with a purely natural explanation. The scribes and Pharisees continually made this error. When will we accept that it is only when we humbly approach him with gratitude for who he is that his Holy Spirit rushes upon us with an understanding that we cannot put into words?

Tuesday of the Third Week of Easter
John 6:30–35

When the crowd asked Jesus for a sign he could perform so that they might believe in him, they mentioned the manna that their ancestors had received in the desert. Jesus responded, "I am the bread of life. Whoever comes to me will never hunger, and whoever believes in me will never thirst."

Those of us who have received him in Holy Communion have received the bread of life. Are you aware of your hunger and thirst being satisfied? Certainly, one can receive Holy Communion and remain physically hungry. The hunger that his body and blood satisfies is our hunger for him. All our appetites demonstrate how incomplete we are in ourselves. They are expressions of our underlying appetite for that eternal union with him that we call heaven. One day we will fully recognize the taste of heaven we had whenever we received him in the Eucharist.

Thursday of the Third Week of Easter
John 6:44–51

Jesus says, "No one can come to me unless the Father who sent me draws him and I will raise him up on the last day. . . . Your ancestors ate the manna in the desert, but they died; this is the bread that comes down from heaven so that one may eat and not die. I am the living bread that comes down from heaven; whoever eats this bread will live forever; and the bread I will give is my Flesh for the life of the world."

We have known many people who have received the Holy Eucharist and have died. The life our Lord speaks of is eternal life. Our daily challenges, our skirmishes with evil and virtue, are not matters of life and death—they are matters of eternal life and eternal death. It is for this reason that we Catholics long for Eucharistic viaticum before we die. It is divine food for the journey to eternity.

Friday of the Third Week of Easter
John 6:52–59

John 6:52 describes how the Jews quarreled among themselves, saying "How can this man give us his flesh to eat? Jesus replied, "Amen, amen, I say to you, unless you eat the flesh of the Son of Man and drink his blood, you do not have life in you. Whoever eats my flesh and drinks my blood has eternal life and I will raise him up on the last day. For my flesh is true food and my blood is true drink."

If his listeners were mistakenly taking him too literally, he could easily have clarified the matter for them. He was not talking about cannibalism, though some have thought so. He was speaking of a sublime mystery. He was speaking of the living sign of his Passion that the Eucharist was to be. The appearance of bread and wine on the altar tells the story. That his body gave of its blood to the death remains the memorial of his infinite love for us that we celebrate at Mass.

Saturday of the Third Week of Easter
John 6:60–69

Many of the Lord's disciples found his words about the Eucharist to be more than they could take. "Does this shake your faith?" he asked them. He told them that his words were spirit and life. But he knew that they weren't ready to believe. When so many disciples left him, he turned to the Twelve and asked if they wanted to leave also. Simon Peter, as usual, spoke for the rest and said, "Lord, to whom shall we go? You have the words of eternal life. We have come to believe; we are convinced that you are God's holy one." Now they didn't understand how they could or should eat his body and drink his blood any more than those who had left him. But they trusted him without understanding because they loved him.

If Jesus were only speaking figuratively, he could easily have called the others back to tell them that he didn't mean it literally. But he did mean it literally. He demonstrates here how he became incarnate, uniting himself with us bodily in this most personal of unions.

Monday of the Fourth Week of Easter
John 10:1–10

Jesus said that whoever does not bring the sheep through the gate is a thief and a robber. He who enters through the gate is the shepherd of the sheep. The gatekeeper opens the gate for him and the sheep recognize his voice. But they will not follow a stranger. Jesus is the gate and those who preceded him were thieves and robbers. The sheep did not follow them. Whoever enters through him will be saved. Thieves come to steal and slaughter, but he came that they might have life and have it abundantly.

Today we hear many voices so contrary to his, promising anything and everything. But ultimately they don't deliver. Only those with faith recognize his voice. Just as his listeners did not easily understand him until he explained in fuller detail, so today he explains more fully by means of the authority he has given only to his Church.

Wednesday of the Fourth Week of Easter
John 12:44–50

Jesus said, "Whoever believes in me believes not only in me but also in the one who sent me, and whoever sees me sees the one who sent me. I came into the world as light so that everyone who believes in me might not remain in the darkness." Despite the passive aggression of his listeners, he offered no hostility in return. He said, "If anyone hears my words and does not observe them, I do not condemn him, for I did not come to condemn but to save the world." He said it is the Word that the Father has given him to speak that will condemn those who reject it.

Today that Word is still with us, and yet our secular media would have us believe that the world remains in darkness. But the worldwide influence of the Catholic Church for over two thousand years still offers light to those who choose to see.

Feast of Sts. Philip and James, Apostles

Thursday of the Fourth Week of Easter
John 14:6–14

Jesus tells his apostles at the last supper that no one comes to the Father except through him. So Philip says, "Lord, show us the Father, and that will be enough for us." But Jesus responds, "Philip, after I've been with you all this time, you still do not know me? Whoever has seen me has seen the Father. How can you say, 'Show us the Father?' . . . Believe me that I am in the Father and the Father is in me, or else, believe because of the works I do."

Philip didn't even realize how shallow his faith was and how little he understood. Our Lord then almost pleads with him to believe—for his own sake. If Philip, who was with him daily, could not hear him, what about us? All the more reason to humbly listen to him as he speaks to us through his Church.

Friday of the Fourth Week of Easter
John 14:1–6

Jesus prepared his apostles for the prospect of his leaving them, assuring them that he would come back again and take them to himself. "Where I am going," he said, "you know the way." Thomas responded, "Master, we do not know where you are going; how can we know the way?" Jesus responded, "I am the way, the truth, and the life. No one comes to the Father except through me." Of course, at the time they didn't know what he was about to endure for them. We do and we hear his words in the context of his passion, death, and resurrection. Still, how often do they grab hold of us?

The apostles did see Jesus again after his Resurrection, and later he did come back for them. But except for John, it was after each of them was martyred. Just as he was the Way for them, so he is for us—but not without the cross in our lives!

Saturday of the Fourth Week of Easter
John 14:7–14

Jesus told the Twelve that if they really knew him, they would know his Father also and that they had seen the Father through Jesus. Philip said, "Lord, show us the Father and that will be enough for us." Jesus responded, "Philip, after I have been with you all this time, and you still don't know me? Whoever has seen me has seen the Father. How can you say, 'Show us the Father?' Believe me that I am in the Father and the Father is in me, or else, believe because of the works that I do." Notice how upset the Lord had become because of Philip's lack of understanding. These were the men he had set aside for special instruction, and on the night before Jesus' death and they didn't seem to have a clue.

It was crucial that they understood his relationship with the Father—and crucial for us, who were to learn from them. "Because I go to the Father, whatever you ask in my name, I will do," he said. The question for us is: Do we have a clue?

Fifth Sunday of Easter • Year B
John 15:1–8

Jesus told the Twelve, "I am the vine and you are the branches. He who lives in me and I in him, will produce abundantly, for apart from me you can do nothing." Of course, he wasn't speaking only of them. He was speaking of you and me as well. How often do we think of our connectedness to him? To see a dead branch cut off from its source is to see us if we are in mortal sin. But when we focus on him, we are most alive. He said that his Father is glorified by our bearing much fruit, so we are capable of glorifying the Father. This means that we can please him and that he wants to take pleasure in us being the people he designed us to be. And he designed us to love him above all else.

Monday of the Fifth Week of Easter
John 14:21–26

Jesus said to his apostles, "Whoever has my commandments and observes them is the one who loves me." And later he said, "The Advocate, the Holy Spirit whom the Father will send in my name—he will teach you everything and remind you of all that I told you." So observing his commandments is how we love him. This can be a consolation when we don't feel very loving.

Of course, observing his commandments means putting him first and ourselves second. Notice how completely turned around this is from what our culture tells us about love. In our culture all the attention is put on ourselves and how we feel. It's a far cry from the images of Good Friday. But it is only from Good Friday that the world will ever truly know how to love.

Tuesday of the Fifth Week of Easter
John 14:27–31a

Jesus said to his disciples, "Peace I leave with you; my peace I give to you. Not as the world gives do I give it to you. Do not let your hearts be troubled or afraid." He then spoke of the joy of returning to the Father, and that the world must know that he loves the Father and that he does as the Father has commanded him.

When we look at his broken body on the cross, his love for the Father is there for the world to see. His obedience furnishes us with the greatest lesson ever taught. To love as he loves brings a peace that can be found nowhere else. It is by embracing the crosses in our lives that we express our love for him in return for all that he has given us. It is through such sacrificial love for him that we will know his peace and know who we are.

Friday of the Fifth Week of Easter
John 15:12–17

Jesus said to his disciples, "This is my commandment: love one another as I have loved you. No one has greater love than this, to lay down one's life for one's friends." He said that he called them friends because he had told them everything he had heard from the Father. "It was not you who chose me, but I who chose you and appointed you to go and bear fruit."

You who are reading this—you exist. You are who you are by his deliberate choice. Everything about you—your personality, your talents, your limitations, the grace that enables you to believe, your volatile temper, your disordered sexuality, your penchant for control, or whatever your cross happens to be— everything is a matter of his design. He has disclosed himself to you and has given his very life. What do you choose in reply? Is there any good in your life that you could possibly withhold from him?

Saturday of the Fifth Week of Easter
John 15:18–21

Jesus told his disciples, "If you find that the world hates you, know that it hated me before you. If you belonged to the world, it would love you as its own; the reason it hates you is that you do not belong to the world. But I chose you out of the world." He reminded them that the slave is no greater than his master. If they hated him, they will hate his followers.

This has been the case for his followers ever since. Strange as it may seem, the response of the world to the manifestation of divine love in its midst is hatred. Yet the Lord allows evil in the world so that a greater good may come of it. Certainly, this applies to his Passion. As horrible as it was, it provided us with the greatest act of love we have ever known. And by our share in his Passion through the crosses in our lives, we will grow in love in ways we never could have imagined without them.

Sixth Sunday of Easter • Year B
John 15:9–17

Jesus told the Twelve, "As the Father has loved me, so I have loved you." Let's put this familiar passage in the present tense. "As the Father loves me, so I love you." It sounds more direct, doesn't it? The night before he died, Jesus spoke of his love for us. On the next day he said it with actions rather than words. Transcending time, his self-gift on the cross redeemed those who came before, those who were present there, and those who would come after, including you and me. At Mass the priest does not create a new sacrifice. If he did, it would do nothing for us because the priest is only human. No, he offers the same sacrifice that Jesus offered, providing us with the presence of that divine act of love in our own time, touching our own lives in the present, and offering us his own body and blood as food to nourish us with now. "As the Father loves me, so I love you."

Feast of St. Matthias, Apostle

Monday of the Sixth Week of Easter
John 15:26–16:4a

When Jesus promised that the advocate would come, he warned the disciples that they would be expelled from the synagogues. The hour would come when they would be killed as an act of worship by ignorant people.

Why does God allow this to be so? Why not have everyone be of an accepting mindset? But such is not God's design. He did not program us to be benign automatons. We can kill the apostles and the prophets who came before them. We can even persecute and put to death the Son of God. Who is this unfathomable being that he allows such evil to rear its wrath upon the sacred? He is Father, Son, and Holy Spirit, who transcends the universe and yet is imaged in our very DNA. Because we know the Father and the Son, we revel in such mystery.

The Advocate has indeed come upon us.

Tuesday of the Sixth Week of Easter
John 16:5–11

Jesus told his disciples that he was returning to the one who sent him. Having said it, he knew the grief they felt. He assured them that this was good for them since the advocate would come only at his departure.

Jesus recognized the pain his words brought to those who were closest to him. It was not his intention to hurt them. He loved them, after all. But he knew better than they what was best for them. And time has certainly proved that to be true. We tend to think of our current difficulties and fears as lasting forever. He knows what a short duration they will actually last. He also knows the glory awaiting us if we just trust him. Moreover, it is the presence of the advocate among us, the Holy Spirit, that gives this moment between you and me the meaning it has.

Wednesday of the Sixth Week of Easter
John 16:12–15

In John 16:12, Jesus told his disciples that he had much more to tell them than they could bear but that the Holy Spirit would later guide them to all truth. "He will not speak on his own," he said, "but will speak what he hears, and will declare to you the things that are coming."

When Jesus said that he had much more to tell, his words rang through the centuries. The spirit of truth guides his Church still. When he ascended to heaven he left a small group of followers; today the Catholic Church covers most of the world. It is the presence of the Spirit that has kept the Church consistent and one in its teaching regardless of the upheavals in each generation. Through the teaching authority of the Church he still has much more to tell us. How willing are we to listen?

Solemnity of the Ascension of the Lord

Thursday of the Sixth Week of Easter
Mark 16:15–20

Jesus said to the Eleven, "'Go into the whole world and proclaim the good news to all creation. The one who believes in it and accepts baptism will be saved; the one who refuses to believe in it will be condemned.' Then after speaking to them, the Lord Jesus was taken up into heaven and took his seat at God's right hand."

Notice he didn't say, "The one who believes will be saved." He said the one who believes and accepts baptism will be saved. He gave them the command of word *and* sacrament. This was the case from the earliest days of the Church. An abundance of evidence shows that the early Church did not consist of the word alone. What one finds in the early Church is still found in the Catholic Church today.

Saturday of the Sixth Week of Easter
John 16:23b–28

Jesus told his disciples, "I give you my assurance, whatever you ask the Father, he will give you in my name. Until now you have not asked for anything in my name. Ask and you shall receive that your joy may be full." He was not giving them a shortcut or sure-fire technique for maneuvering God into giving them what they want. Before he became incarnate, the Jewish people asked the Father in prayer for what they needed and he heard their prayers. But now they know the Son and are his friends. The Father's love for them is colored by this. God has never been a big vending machine in the sky. He is the God of love. He has always responded when people have come to him in love. But now our love is infused with our identification with Jesus—and our joy is full!

Seventh Sunday of Easter • Year B
John 17:11b–19

Jesus prayed to the Father for the Twelve, gathered with him in the upper room the night before he died. "O Father most holy, protect them with your name which you have given me, that they may be one, even as we are one. . . . Consecrate them by means of truth—'Your word is truth.'"

Often on our forums, when people are discerning what Christian church to belong to, they cite the friendliness of the parishioners or the personality of the pastor or what they don't like about other churches they have encountered. But so often they miss the one quality that is absolutely essential. They fail to ask if it teaches the complete truth. Yet Jesus was so concerned that his followers be consecrated in truth. Only one Church has taught the same, consistent understanding of Scripture throughout the world for over two thousand years—because he himself consecrated it in truth.

Monday of the Seventh Week of Easter
John 16:29–33

The disciples said to Jesus, "Now you are talking plainly, and not in any figure of speech. Now we realize that you know everything and that you do not need to have anyone question you. Because of this we believe that you came from God." Jesus answered them, "Do you believe now? Behold, the hour is coming and has arrived when each of you will be scattered to his own home and you will leave me alone."

They thought they understood, but our Lord said, "Not so fast!" He is the Eternal Mystery, after all. We don't always feel that comfortable with mystery. We want it all out there. Eventually the disciples learned that trusting his love for them was enough. Not all of us are there yet. We need more quiet time before the tabernacle and crucifix.

Tuesday of the Seventh Week of Easter
John 17:1–11a

Jesus was with his apostles in the upper room the night before he died. He prayed, "Father, the hour has come. Give glory to your Son, so that your son may glorify you. . . . I revealed your name to those whom you gave me out of the world. . . . Now they know that everything you gave me is from you because the words you gave to me I have given to them, and they accepted them and truly understood that I came from you, and they believe that you sent me."

In his most intimate time with his apostles our Lord revealed his intimacy with the Father. His Father means everything to him and he wanted to share this with them. While they can't take it all in at the time, they eventually do—which is how we know about it. It remains for us to accept such intimacy by having daily time with him. To do so will eventually ravish us.

Wednesday of the Seventh Week of Easter
John 17:11b–19

Jesus prayed for those entrusted to his care. "I do not ask that you take them out of the world," he said, "but that you keep them from the Evil One. . . . They do not belong to the world any more than I belong to the world. Consecrate them in the truth. Your word is truth."

Jesus consecrates us in truth to protect us from the evil one, the prince of lies. Every sin is a lie. It puts us first and God second. To be consecrated in truth is to be totally dedicated to God.

That we have sinned and sinned again shows us how easy the lie is. It is only when we are honest about our lying ways that repentance is possible. Such is always the result of his grace and our willingness to accept it. He knows better than we how weak we are. But his love is strong and ever near.

Thursday of the Seventh Week of Easter
John 17:20–26

Jesus lifted up his eyes to heaven in the presence of the apostles and prayed, "I pray not only for these, but also for those who will believe in me through their word, so that they all may be one, as you Father, are in me and I in you." And a little later, he said, "Father, they are your gift to me. I wish that where I am they also may be with me, that they may see the glory that you gave me, because you loved me before the foundation of the world."

How does it feel to be the subject of the Son's prayer to his Father at the Last Supper? He is speaking here about you and me. He wants us to be where he is. He considers us the Fathers' gift to him. On the cross he showed us just how much he treasures us. And it is through the crosses in our lives that we are able to show how much he means to us.

Friday of the Seventh Week of Easter
John 21:15–19

Jesus said to Simon Peter, "Simon, son of John, do you love me more than these?" Simon Peter answered him, "Yes, Lord, you know that I love you." He asked him the same question two more times. The third time Peter was distressed and answered, "Lord, you know everything; you know that I love you." After each of Peter's answers, Jesus told him to feed and tend his sheep. Then Jesus told him that in old age he would lose the independence of his youth. "Someone else will dress you and lead you where you do not want to go."

Jesus was showing us what he expected of any disciple. Do we love him—not just as our God, but as our friend? Is he on our mind frequently—not only when we want something, when we are mainly concerned with ourselves—but with him in what he wants? How much does he matter to us in the choices we make each day?

Pentecost Sunday • Year B
John 20:19–23

On Easter Sunday evening the apostles locked themselves in the upper room since were still fearful for their lives because of their association with Jesus. Suddenly Jesus stood in their midst. "Peace be with you," he said. Then he showed them the scars on his hands and his side and said, "As the Father has sent me, so I send you." Then he breathed on them and said, "Receive the Holy Spirit. If you forgive men's sins, they are forgiven them; if you hold them bound, they are held bound." One really has to work at not recognizing the power to forgive sins that Jesus gave to his apostles in this passage. When people ask why Catholics have to confess to a priest to have their sins forgiven, this is where it comes from. It was Jesus' idea, and it is through the power of the Holy Spirit that it is possible. When the priest raises his hand in absolution, the penitent sees his hand, but it is really the nail-scarred hand of Jesus that is giving absolution.

Monday of the Eighth Week
of Ordinary Time • Mark 10:17–27

When a man asked Jesus what he must do to inherit eternal life, Jesus looked at him with love and said, "Go, sell what you have and give to the poor and you will have treasure in heaven; then come and follow me." The man was crushed because he couldn't part with his many possessions. Jesus then commented twice on how hard it is for the rich to enter the kingdom of heaven.

The question for us is: To what are you most attached? Never mind wealth and status. What about your work, your health and vitality, your family, your life as you are living it right now? What would be the most difficult to give up? No matter how good it is, it is only a spark of the flame of its source. And that good is the Lord .

Tuesday of the Eighth Week
of Ordinary Time • Mark 10:28–31

Peter said to Jesus, "We have given up everything and followed you." Jesus acknowledged that no one who has given up house or brothers or sisters or mother or father or children or lands for his sake and for the sake of the gospel will not receive a hundred times more in the present age—along with persecutions— and eternal life in the age to come.

To give up all in order to have him in this life will mean having the consolation of his favor, but it will include the cross. For the apostles, except for John, it was to include martyrdom. For us it means enduring the crosses that each one of us has. What are we going to get for following him? We will have him. The better we know him, the more we understand that he is more than enough.

Wednesday of the Eighth Week
of Ordinary Time • Mark 10:32–45

James and John asked Jesus if they could sit, one and his right and the other at his left, when he would come into his glory. He responded in a gentle way by asking them if they could drink of the cup from which he was to drink. They both answered that they could—not really knowing what he meant. Then the others became indignant, fearing they would be losing out.

Jesus then explained the dynamics of love. Love demands that the lover be centered on the one loved and not on oneself. It sounds fairly obvious, but not for the self-centered, and you and I have succumbed to such self-centeredness more often than we care to acknowledge. It is Jesus himself, hanging on the cross, who shows us what love is. May we never lose sight of it.

Feast of the Visitation

Thursday of the Eighth Week
of Ordinary Time • Luke 1:39–56

In Luke 1:39, we read, "Mary set out and traveled to the hill country in haste to a town of Judah, where she entered the house of Zechariah and greeted Elizabeth." Here we have the most sublime meeting between two human beings in the history of the race. It is a meeting of mothers filled with the Holy Spirit. Talk about liberated women! Elizabeth says, "How is it that the mother of my Lord should come to me?" And some question why Catholics call Mary the Mother of God. Ask Elizabeth.

Mary says that her soul magnified the lord. Like a magnifying glass she makes the Lord more visible by her fidelity as well as by her offspring. The effects of that meeting reach out to all eternity, and yet the passage ends in understatement: Mary remained with her about three months and then returned home.

Saturday of the Eighth Week
of Ordinary Time • Mark 11:27–33

Some scribes and chief priests approached Jesus in the temple area and demanded to know by what authority he based his public behavior. He responded that he would tell them if they could tell him whether John's baptism was of divine or merely human origin. It was an honest question. But they were not prepared to answer it because it would have been self-condemning, since they had not supported John's mission. Yet they dared not counter the popular belief that John was a prophet of God. So they refused to answer, and Jesus refused also. John's message was for the people to do penance and reform their lives. The chief priests, scribes, and Pharisees were in no way going to do this. This is why Jesus became so threatening to them. This is also why his Church threatens many even today. Conversion usually comes about when we are hurting and therefore more open—not when we're riding high and inclined to be self-absorbed. A word to the wise!

Trinity Sunday • Year B • Matthew 28:16–20

Jesus summoned the Eleven to the top of a mountain. There he said, "Full authority has been given to me both in heaven and on earth; go therefore, make disciples of all nations. Baptize them in the name of the Father and of the Son and of the Holy Spirit. Teach them to carry out everything I have commanded you. And know that I am with you always, until the end of the world!" His first command was to baptize and then to teach. They were to make disciples by sacrament and word. The people created in the image and likeness of the Trinity were to be baptized in the name of the Trinity. It is ironic that we so often think of the Trinity as being unknowable when we are immersed in it. Everything we know bears evidence of its Triune Creator. Our very hearts beat in the name of the Father and of the Son and of the Holy Spirit.

Monday of the Ninth Week
of Ordinary Time • Mark 12:1–12

In speaking to the chief priests and scribes, Jesus told a parable about a man who planted a vineyard, dug a wine press, and built a tower that he leased out. Later he sent a servant to the tenants to obtain some of the produce. But they seized and beat the servant and even killed his son, whom he later sent. Jesus asked his audience how the owner should respond. They answered that he should put the tenants to death and give the operation to others.

When Jesus then quoted from Scripture: "The stone that the builders rejected has become the cornerstone," they realized that he considered them the tenants and he the Son. Unknowingly, they had convicted themselves.

We need to pray for the wisdom to see those areas in which we are quick to condemn others over deeds we perform time and again, and then we need to repent.

Wednesday of the Ninth Week
of Ordinary Time • Mark.12:18–27

Some Sadducees, who refused to believe in the Resurrection, challenged Jesus with a hypothetical situation in which a woman was the widow of seven brothers who died consecutively. At the Resurrection, whose wife would she be? Our Lord responded that they were misled because they knew neither Scripture nor the power of God. He explained that after the husband and wife rise from the dead, they neither marry nor are given in marriage. In this they are like angels.

In these readings, we frequently encounter people who challenge Jesus without realizing just who he really is. In this instance the Sadducees are intent on justifying their lack of belief in the Resurrection. They're not much concerned about the truth. Jesus takes the opportunity to speak of heaven as union with God and the fulfillment of every human desire. We all need to listen to him about his plans for us.

Thursday of the Ninth Week
of Ordinary Time • Mark 12:28b–34

When a scribe asked Jesus for the first commandment, he responded, "Hear, O Israel, the Lord our God is Lord alone! You shall love the Lord your God with all your heart, with all your soul, with all your mind and with all your strength." Besides being the *shema*, the prayer that all devout Jews pray every day, Jesus' answer also mirrors the vows of religious life.

The vow of poverty offers to God all one's possessions. The vow of celibate chastity offers one's sexuality and all relationships. The vow of obedience offers one's will and power of choice. These vows comprise the totality of human life. Religious life reminds us that everyone is called to surrender his entire life to God's supreme dominion over him: possessions, sexuality—whether celibate or married— and choice. We owe God such acknowledgment simply because in his goodness he is who he is!

Saturday of the Ninth Week
of Ordinary Time • Mark 12:38–44

Jesus said, "Be on guard against the scribes, who like to parade around in their robes and accept marks of respect in public. These men devour the savings of widows and recite long prayers for appearance's sake; it is they who will receive the severest sentence." He observed the wealthy putting sizeable amounts of money into the coin collection box, but one widow put in two copper coins worth about one cent. He said that she put in more the all the rest because they gave out of their abundance, but she gave all she had to live on. Of course, the scribes and the wealthy were not likely to dwell on their self-absorption—still less that God was aware of it. But Jesus knew it all. And he still does. We do well to ask him to reveal to us our acts of hypocrisy while we still have time to repent of them.

Corpus Christi Sunday • Year B
Mark 14:12–16, 22–26

When the Twelve were all present for the Passover supper, Jesus took bread, blessed and broke it and said, "Take this; this is my body." Then he took a cup of wine, blessed it and said, "This is my blood, the blood of the covenant, to be poured out on behalf of many." This was, of course, in anticipation of what was to happen the next day on Calvary—though the apostles didn't yet know that. There on Calvary he was to reveal to us mortal ones more about who God is than was ever revealed before or after. That God would choose to suffer and die for us, whom he created from nothing, reveals to our feeble intellects something of the magnificence of who he is and how much he values us. The Eucharist personalizes his Passion in that through it he comes to us personally, dwelling within our souls and our bodies.

Memorial of St. Barnabas, Apostle

Monday of the Tenth Week
of Ordinary Time • Matthew 5:1–12

Jesus went up a mountain before a large crowd and began to teach them, saying, "Blessed are the poor in spirit, for theirs is the Kingdom of heaven." He then continued with several other blesseds. "Blessed are they who mourn . . . blessed are the meek . . ." and so forth. These are the eight Beatitudes—eight ways of being happy. What is it about such things that would make us happy, especially being persecuted for justice's sake?

The beatitudes are expressions of concern for others. They are eight ways of showing love. Our Blessed Lord is telling us that happiness lies only in doing what we were designed for. We were designed to love God above all and to love each other for his sake. When we do this we are most truly ourselves. Better yet, we are most truly his. He promises that our reward in heaven will be great. Of course it will. We will finally fully know his divine embrace.

Tuesday of the Tenth Week
of Ordinary Time • Matthew 5:13–16

Jesus said to his disciples, "You are the salt of the earth. But if salt loses its taste, with what can it be seasoned? It is no longer good for anything. . . . You are the light of the world. Your light must shine before others that they may see your good deeds and glorify your heavenly Father."

In many ways we Catholics blend in with the greater population. Culturally, we are very much the same. What distinguishes us—other than the fact that we attend the local Catholic church? Do we say grace in restaurants? Do we dress more modestly than the current norm? Are we found at daily Mass? Are we openly pro-life with those who would disagree? How willing are we to risk disapproval for our commitment to our faith? How much do we love him? Now—what are your Catholic answers?

Wednesday of the Tenth Week
of Ordinary Time • Matthew 5:17–19

Jesus said to his disciples, "Do not think that I have come to abolish the law or the prophets. I have come not to abolish but to fulfill." The Ten Commandments, the expression of liturgical prayer, the liturgical calendar, blessings, incense, water, wine, priesthood, days of fast, sacrifice—all these aspects of ancient Judaism remain in his Church but are transformed and given completion by his Passion and Resurrection.

"Blessed are you, Lord God of all creation, through your goodness we have this bread to offer.... Blessed are you, Lord God of all creation, through your goodness we have this wine to offer." These are Jewish ways of praying. Nowhere will you find more of Christianity's Jewish roots than in Catholicism. Blessed are those who recognize the Old Law's fulfillment here.

JUNE 14, 2012

Thursday of the Tenth Week
of Ordinary Time • Matthew 5:20–26

Jesus said, "I tell you, unless your righteousness surpasses that of the scribes and Pharisees, you will not enter the kingdom of heaven. You have heard that it was said to our ancestors, 'You shall not kill; and whoever kills will be liable to judgment.' But I say to you, whoever is angry with his brother will be liable to judgment." If such is the case, one must reconcile before approaching the altar.

The Old Law was good as far as it went. But here again we find our Lord going deeper than the Old Law had done by regulating external behavior. Jesus is concerned with what precedes the external act in the mind of the individual. If one wills the harm of his brother, he has violated the Law even if he has not yet laid a hand on his brother. Such evil intent is totally incompatible with our worship and our love for God.

Solemnity of the Sacred Heart of Jesus

Friday of the Tenth Week
of Ordinary Time • John 19:31–37

The soldiers broke the legs of the two who were crucified with Jesus. But seeing that Jesus was already dead, one soldier thrust his lance into his side, and immediately blood and water flowed out. The early Church Fathers interpreted the water to symbolize baptism and the blood the Eucharist. They saw these life-giving streams as the graces that produced a second Eve, the Church, from a second Adam, unconscious on the cross.

It is in this physical piercing of his heart that the early Church honored the heart of Jesus as the symbol of his love for the people for whom he willingly shed his blood. In most societies the heart symbolizes the core of who one is. *Core* comes from the Latin for heart. From the core of who Jesus is, he loves us. This is what the Catholic devotion to the Sacred Heart of Jesus is all about—who Jesus really is and how much we matter to him.

Memorial of the Immaculate Heart of Mary

Saturday of the Tenth Week
of Ordinary Time • Luke 2:41–51

Today we celebrate the Immaculate Heart of Mary—which means recalling the basic goodness of the woman God chose to be the Mother of his Son. Scripture throws a very revealing light on her. The following Scripture quotes readily show anyone with a basic familiarity with the life of Jesus how important she was in his life.

To the angel Gabriel she said (Luke 1:38): "Let what you have said be done to me." When Jesus had been lost for three days (Luke 2:48): "My child, why have you done this to us? See how worried your father and I have been, looking for you." When Jesus worked his first miracle at her request (John 2:4–5): "They have no wine." And later, "Do whatever he tells you." And (John 19:26) from the cross Jesus told John: "This is your mother." And then to Mary, "Woman, this is your son."

No wonder she means so very much to us.

Eleventh Sunday of Ordinary Time
Year B • Mark 4:26–34

Jesus said, "This is how it is with the kingdom of God; it is as if a man were to scatter seed on the land and would sleep and rise night and day and through it all the seed would sprout and grow, he knows not how. Of its own accord the land yields fruit, first the blade, then the ear, then the full grain in the ear. And when the grain is ripe, he wields the sickle at once, for the harvest has come."

The ways of nature and the ways of his kingdom both flow from his will, and both are intended for our benefit. Long after the growing of food is no longer necessary, we will be enjoying the kingdom. It is a kingdom of his love, which, like grain, increases in our lives while we are sleeping and while we are awake. How, we do not know. First we are born. Then we grow to adulthood, carrying our crosses in response to his love. Finally, we die and are born to him forever.

Monday of the Eleventh Week
of Ordinary Time • Matthew 5:38–42

Jesus said, "You have heard that it was said, an eye for an eye and a tooth for a tooth. But I say to you, offer no resistance to one who is evil. When someone strikes you on your right cheek, turn the other one to him as well."

It is important to recognize the hyperbole here, the exaggeration to make a point. Our Lord's concern in this matter was not that we become doormats for other people. This wouldn't be any better for them than it would be for us. Actually, he wasn't passive in such a situation. He spoke up for himself in John 18:23 when a guard slapped him in the face. He certainly wasn't passive when he encountered the buying and selling in the temple. His concern is that we subordinate strict justice to generous charity. Smothering others with kindness actually works when our motivation is true concern for them. It's all a matter of love.

Tuesday of the Eleventh Week
of Ordinary Time • Matthew 5:43–48

Jesus said to his disciples, "You have heard it said, 'You shall love your neighbor and hate your enemy.' But I say to you, love your enemies and pray for those who persecute you." The Jews had a very real disdain for pagan foreigners, whom they saw as a threat to the purity of their race and religion. But as the Messiah, Jesus came not only for the chosen people but for the whole world as well! He was the first to teach not tolerance but genuine love for everyone. "Neighbor" meant that everyone was a member of one's tribe, including tax collectors and pagans.

For Jesus one must love everyone enough to speak the truth to him as he did—even to relatives and the people one works with. The more we love them, the less uncomfortable we will be with them! The truth cuts, but ultimately it heals.

Wednesday of the Eleventh Week
of Ordinary Time • Matthew 6:1–6, 16–18

Jesus warned us not to perform religious deeds in order that people may see them. "When you give alms," he said, "do not blow a trumpet before you as the hypocrites do in the synagogues and in the streets to win the praise of others. Amen, I say to you, they have received their reward." In telling his disciples this, of course, he is telling us as well. We are to give to the poor in secret. But his point here is not about doing things secretly.

There are other passages in which he encourages us to let our good works be seen as an example to others. His concern is that we be centered on God and not ourselves. To do good and even holy things for selfish reasons betrays our lack of love for him. The clock is ticking. Our days here are limited. There is only so much more time for accepting the inconvenience of truly loving those he puts in our path. Let's use that time as he would.

Thursday of the Eleventh Week
of Ordinary Time • Matthew 6:7–15

Jesus told his disciples that when they pray, they are not to babble like the pagans, who think they will be heard because of their many words. "Do not be like them!" he says. "Your heavenly Father knows your needs before you ask him."

What about the rosary and the litanies? Do these qualify as the babbling of many words? Not at all— they aren't babbling. To babble is to make incoherent noises. The prayers we repeat during the rosary are quite coherent. The same is true of litanies. But more than that, they are ways of saying, "I love you, I love you, I love you." The Lord never tires of hearing all the many ways we have of expressing this.

We don't pray to inform God of anything. We pray to express what matters most to us: that he matters most, that we need him, that we are sorry for our offenses against him, and that we are grateful. Amen.

Friday of the Eleventh Week
of Ordinary Time • Matthew 6:19–23

Jesus cautioned about storing up treasures on earth that can decay or be stolen. Instead, store up treasures in heaven. "Where your treasure is," he said, "there also will your heart be." He also advised that the eye is the lamp of the body. If your eye is sound, the whole body will be filled with light. But if not, how great will the darkness be!

In other words, the sense of proper proportions comes from a sound mind, which he likens to a body filled with light. If we are centered on God, then he is our treasure and has our heart. If not, how dark will the darkness in which we live be! There's only one choice. We choose him first or we choose ourselves. Which will it be?

Saturday of the Eleventh Week
of Ordinary Time • Matthew 6:24–34

Jesus states that we cannot serve two masters. To try is to end up serving one and not the other. We can only have one priority at a time. He is zeroing in on control freaks here. "O weak in faith! Stop worrying over questions like, 'What are we to eat or what are we to drink, or what are we to wear? . . .' Your heavenly Father knows all that you need. Seek first his kingship over you, his way of holiness and all these things will be given you besides." Too often people pride themselves on being responsible, when in reality, they are really very self-serving. When things then don't work, they feel sorry for themselves. Of course, I am speaking of those other control freaks—not you and me. But certainly even we can learn from their mistakes.

Twelfth Sunday of Ordinary Time
Year B • Luke 1:57–66, 80

When the infant John the Baptist was being circumcised, the rabbi was about to name him Zechariah after his father. But Elizabeth, his mother, insisted that he be called John. His father, who had been struck dumb for his unbelief, confirmed this by writing "John" on a tablet. Immediately, Zechariah was able to speak and the people knew that "surely the hand of the Lord was with John."

They were taken back by this manifestation that God was present and had deliberate plans for the child. This is just as true when a child is baptized—except that at baptism the Holy Spirit rushes upon the child with sanctifying grace. Nuclear fission would seem like child's play if we could see what actually takes place in the soul of that little body. Today as we celebrate the birth of St. John the Baptist, let us give thanks for the gift of our baptism and our life in Christ.

Tuesday of the Twelfth Week
of Ordinary Time • Matthew 7:6, 12–14

Jesus said to his disciples, "Do to others whatever you would have them do to you. This is the Law and the Prophets." We're all familiar with this "Golden Rule," as it has come to be called. It's an easy one to understand. It requires that we at least theoretically consider the other person's situation. To do this asks us to acknowledge that the other person is worth at least as much as ourselves. I say "at least" because if we truly love the other person, we may find ourselves putting his welfare above our own. Parents often do this for their children. Our Blessed Lord certainly did this for us. It's the way of love.

So as I speak these words to you through your radio or computer or the written word, know that I consciously try to keep you in mind as I speak them. I consider you worth the effort. But more importantly, so does the Lord.

Wednesday of the Twelfth Week
of Ordinary Time • Matthew 7:15–20

Jesus told his disciples, "Beware of false prophets, who come to you in sheep's clothing, but underneath are ravenous wolves. By their fruits you shall know them. . . . Every good tree bears good fruit and a rotten tree bears bad fruit." Therefore the kind of person you are will inevitably affect what you do, what you say, and what you take in. In school, Sister used to warn us that we would be affected by the kind of company we kept. Of course this didn't resonate with us at the time. Today I am very much aware of how we influence each other and how subtle the influence can be.

In the past few years I have become aware of how I had been duped for many years by the secular media and how I can't trust most of them now. All the more reason to appreciate such outlets as the *National Catholic Register*, Catholic Answers, and EWTN.

Solemnity of Sts. Peter and Paul, Apostles

Friday of the Twelfth Week
of Ordinary Time • Matthew 16:13–19

Jesus asked his apostles, "Who do you say that I am?" Simon Peter replied, "You are the Christ, the Son of the living God." Jesus said, "Blessed are you, Simon son of Jonah, for flesh and blood have not revealed this to you, but my heavenly Father. And so I say to you, you are Peter, and upon this rock I will build my Church, and the gates of the netherworld shall not prevail against it."

It was to Peter the impetuous, the sinner, to whom the apostles nevertheless deferred, that Jesus gave the keys of the kingdom of heaven. In doing so, he conferred the authority to loose and to bind that has been shared with Linus, Cletus, Clement, and all their successors to the present pope, Benedict XVI. Ours is a Church of sinners who nevertheless can be raised to great holiness by the merits of Jesus on the cross.

Saturday of the Twelfth Week
of Ordinary Time • Matthew 8:5–17

A centurion asked Jesus to cure his servant boy, who was paralyzed and in great pain. Jesus agreed to go and heal him. But the centurion responded that he was not worthy to have Jesus under his roof. He asked Jesus to heal him from afar. Jesus responded that he had never found such faith in all of Israel. The centurion, of course, was a Roman and up to this point not considered a believer. Jesus immediately healed the servant boy. He used the occasion to remark that many from east and west will find a place at the banquet in the kingdom of God, while the natural heirs (meaning the Israelites) will be driven out.

Jesus came for the humble, whoever they are and wherever they are. We will all be surprised one day to see who was the most open to him. No one is unknown to him and no one—absolutely no one—is beyond his love.

Thirteenth Sunday of Ordinary Time
Year B • Mark 5:21–24, 35–43

Jesus cured a woman with a hemorrhage as he proceeded to go to the home of a man named Jairus, whose young daughter had just died. When he arrived, he told the child to get up and she immediately began to walk around the room. He told the parents to give her something to eat. As with so many other miracles he performed, he ordered the people not to let others know about it.

We are so familiar with his miracles that their force remains an abstraction for us. After all, we weren't there. We didn't witness them firsthand. But actually it is not necessary for us to have been there to be moved. For their significance to hit home, all we need to do is recognize the presence of Jesus in our lives. It may be the feel and sound of our heart beating and the realization that he is on the other side of it. Or it may simply be the fact that we believe. The only possible reason for one to believe in him is his deliberate desire to give us such a gift.

JULY 2, 2012

Monday of the Thirteenth Week
of Ordinary Time • Matthew 8:18–22

A scribe approached Jesus and said, "Teacher, I will follow you wherever you go." Jesus answered, "Foxes have dens and birds of the sky have nests, but the Son of Man has nowhere to rest his head." Another disciple promised to follow, but first he had to bury his father. Jesus told him to let the burial of the dead be done by those who are not intent on the greater interests of God.

It wasn't that he disregarded such a sacred duty. He was concerned with emphasizing the priority that discipleship demands. To throw in one's lot with him is to trust in him over the world and to let nothing matter more. Such requirements haven't changed since then—except that since you and I have made the scene, they apply to us as well!

Feast of St. Thomas, Apostle

Tuesday of the Thirteenth Week
of Ordinary Time • John 20:24–29

Jesus suddenly stood before his apostles in the upper room as he had done the week before. But this time Thomas, who was previously absent, was present. Even though the others had testified that they had seen Jesus, he stubbornly refused to believe unless, as he said, he could see and put his finger into the marks in his hands and put his hand into his side. So Jesus called him forth to do just that. Evidently the death of Jesus had been so traumatic for Thomas that he couldn't bear to get his hopes up, with the accompanying possibility of having to suffer the loss of Jesus a second time. But when faced with the reality of his presence, Thomas, falling prostrate, made the most explicit act of faith in Jesus in all of Scripture: "My Lord and my God!

Wednesday of the Thirteenth Week
of Ordinary Time • Matthew 8:28–34

When Jesus passed through Geracene territory, his presence aggravated some demons who were tormenting two men. The demons immediately asked to be sent into a herd of swine nearby. So Jesus expelled them from the men and did as they requested. The herd then ran into the sea and drowned. When the people of the area heard what had happened, they were frightened and begged him to leave—as if his power over evil was what should be feared. This is the way of evil. Satan is the champion of the lie. He always displays evil as good. So even today, the killing of one's unborn child is seen as giving the mother the freedom to choose—without acknowledging the evil horror of the choice.

By sacrificing himself in love on the cross, Jesus turned evil on its head and conquered it. To the degree that we share in that sacrificial love we will conquer evil as well.

Thursday of the Thirteenth Week
of Ordinary Time • Matthew 9:1–8

Jesus entered his own town, where some people brought him a paralytic lying on a stretcher. When he saw their faith he said, "Courage, child, your sins are forgiven." At this some scribes assumed that he was blaspheming. Jesus knew their thinking and said, "Why do you harbor such thoughts? Which is easier to say, 'Your sins are forgiven,' or 'Rise up and walk?' But that you may know that the Son of Man has authority on earth to forgive sins, Rise, pick up your stretcher and go home." He then rose and went home. By showing them his power over flesh and bone, he showed them his power over the spiritual as well. He is God, after all!

But what about us? Which is easier for him to say, "Exist, be substantial," or "I absolve you from your sins in the name of the Father and of the Son and of the Holy Spirit"!?

Friday of the Thirteenth Week
of Ordinary Time • Matthew 9:9–13

When Jesus called Matthew, a tax collector, to follow him and then joined him for dinner at his home, the Pharisees could not understand the company he was keeping.

Of course, being a tax collector for the Romans who kept the Jews under their power, Matthew was seen by his fellow Jews to be somewhat of a traitor. Yet not only did Jesus eat with him in his home, he called him to follow him as an apostle. In doing this, he demonstrated to people all through the ages that no one is beyond his love and concern. He came for everyone. But as with Matthew, to be his follower means to accommodate one's life completely to all that he requires. He who died, preferring nothing to us, deserves that we prefer nothing.

Saturday of the Thirteenth Week
of Ordinary Time • Matthew 9:14–17

When John the Baptist's disciples asked Jesus why his disciples didn't have to fast while they did, Jesus told them that is it not appropriate for wedding guests to fast while at the wedding. Later, after the wedding, there will be time for fasting. They didn't realize that Jesus was God and that his visit on earth was for a limited time. Not only were his disciples to fast one day, but many of them would be put to death on his account. Of course, they were not prepared to understand all this at the time. They just had to take him at his word. This is true of us as well. There are all kinds of questions we would like to ask him—most of them having to do with aspects of our lives that we don't like and don't understand. If we knew what he knows, we'd be satisfied—but we would also forgo the opportunity of expressing the love for him that our trust in him accomplishes.

Tuesday of the Fourteenth Week
of Ordinary Time • Matthew 9:32–38

"A demoniac who could not speak was brought to Jesus, and when the demon was driven out, the mute man spoke." The people were amazed at this. The Gospel says that Jesus went around all the towns and villages, teaching in their synagogues, proclaiming the Gospel of the kingdom, and curing every illness. At the sight of the crowds, his heart was moved with pity for them because they were like sheep without a shepherd.

And this is why he founded his Church. He continues to shepherd his people under the guidance of his vicar on earth, the bishop of Rome. It is significant that the pope's staff is not in the shape of a hook but has a crucifix at its end. It is through the fruit of the Lord's Passion that his sheep are fed—even today. How much do you hunger? How much do you thirst?

Wednesday of the Fourteenth Week of Ordinary Time • Matthew 10:1–7

Jesus summoned the Twelve and gave them authority to drive out unclean spirits and to cure every disease. After instructing them to avoid pagan territory and Samaritan towns, he then sent them out. They were to proclaim the kingdom of heaven to the lost sheep of the house of Israel. His first concern was for his chosen people. God had singled them out for a special relationship with him. Jesus, the Messiah who came from them and for them, was simply acknowledging this. God would never forget his special relationship with them. Even now they remain his chosen people.

But his love is not limited to them. His love is not limited, period. You are the deliberate result of his love. Not only is every hair of you head numbered; so is every beat of your heart! In life and in death you are his.

Thursday of the Fourteenth Week
of Ordinary Time • Matthew 10:7–15

Jesus told his apostles, "As you go, make this proclamation: 'The kingdom of God is at hand.' Cure the sick, raise the dead, cleanse the lepers, drive out demons. Without cost you have received; without cost you are to give. Do not take gold or silver or copper for your belts; no sack for the journey, or a second tunic, or sandals, or walking stick. The laborer deserves his keep. . . . Whoever will not receive you or listen to your words, go outside that house or town and shake the dust from your feet."

Obviously, the word they were preaching was not a message that was watered down so that it could not offend anybody. Nothing about them suggested that they were preaching the good news about an earthly kingdom. Their message was that our true home is heaven, not here, and that he is the only way to get there!

JULY 13, 2012

Friday of the Fourteenth Week
of Ordinary Time • Matthew 10:16–23

Jesus told his apostles that he was sending them out like sheep into the midst of wolves. They were to be wise as serpents and innocent as doves. He warned them that they will be flogged in synagogues and dragged before governors and kings. But they are not to worry about what to say, because when they speak it will be the Spirit of the Father speaking through them. How does that work? How can I be sure that it is the Spirit speaking through me and not my own ideas? When one is in danger and speaks from his heart in defense of his Lord, there is little chance that he is speaking from his ego. Nevertheless, should we be incorrect and misspeak, we have his Church to guide us with the authority it received from him. It gives us a security that we can find nowhere else.

Saturday of the Fourteenth Week
of Ordinary Time • Matthew 10:24–33

Jesus said that no pupil outranks his teacher. But for
the pupil to identify with the teacher means that the
pupil will likely suffer whatever the teacher suffers.
He warns the apostles not to be intimidated by those
who would oppose them. He tells them to proclaim
from the housetops what he has taught them privately.
They are not to fear, for every hair of their heads is
numbered. They are in their Father's care.

He knew full well all those who would oppose his
Church in the years and centuries to come. We tend to
forget that he is very aware of us and our experiences
at all times. Because we can't see him, we assume that
he can't see us. Yet our very existence depends on his
willing it at all times. What he said to his apostles he
says to us who identify with him.

Monday of the Fifteenth Week
of Ordinary Time • Matthew 10:34–11:1

Jesus said to his apostles, "Do not think that I have come to bring peace upon the earth. I have come to bring not peace but the sword." He cautions that one's enemies will be in one's very household. "Whoever loves mother and father more than me is not worthy of me," he said. Nor is one who refuses to take up his cross. No middle ground here! Then he says, "Whoever receives you receives me, and whoever receives me receives the one who sent me."

This is a clear example of our Lord's intention to continue his mission through his Church. "Whoever receives you receives me." He will remain present in the world through his apostles and their successors. The Church will be rocked by strife and even martyrdom—not to mention scandal—but he remains with her and through her offers his cross to whoever will follow. And the cross in our lives leads us directly to him.

Tuesday of the Fifteenth Week
of Ordinary Time • Matthew 11:20–24

Jesus began to reproach the towns where most of his mighty deeds had been done, since they had not repented. "Woe to you, Chorazin! Woe to you, Bethsaida! For if the mighty deeds done in your midst had been done in Tyre and Sidon, they would long ago have repented in sackcloth and ashes. But I tell you, it will be more tolerable for Tyre and Sidon on the Day of Judgment than for you." It's quite evident that while his mercy is infinite, God does expect something of us. His gift of grace does not take our personal responsibility away. Actually, it makes us more responsible. To love is to respond to the beloved.

To make a one-time commitment to him and then expect salvation regardless of future behavior, as some do, is irresponsible and contradicts his expectations of us. We expect more from our friends. Why should he not expect more from us?

Friday of the Fifteenth Week of Ordinary Time • Matthew 12:1–8

The Pharisees complained because Jesus' disciples were picking heads of grain and eating them on the Sabbath. Jesus confounded such casuistry by showing that necessity excused them from the Law. He reminded them of how David and his men had eaten the bread of offering from the temple because he was in great hunger and fleeing for his life. Jesus then said, "I say to you, something greater than the temple is here. . . . For the Son of Man is Lord of the Sabbath."

When one is centered on the Lord and not on oneself, he can let the chips fall where they may. He will have no fear of displeasing the Lord. Even if he should make a mistake, he can be at peace because he is acting from a clean conscience. Besides, he knows that something greater than the temple is here and that he is living his life before the face of a loving God.

Saturday of the Fifteenth Week
of Ordinary Time • Matthew 12:14–21

Jesus was aware of the Pharisees plotting to destroy him. So he withdrew to another place. Still many people followed him, but he continually warned them not to publicize what he was doing for them. When the appointed time came, he would deliberately make himself vulnerable to the enemy. But until then, his ministry was gentle and peaceful as had been prophesized by Isaiah: "He will not contend or cry out, nor will his voice be heard in the streets. The bruised reed he will not crush. . . . In his name, the Gentiles will find hope."

This is where we come in. Even with us today, he comes gently and not by force. We know him by what he was willing to suffer for us. It is by love that he conquers us, not by might—and yet nothing is more powerful. The crucifix is the most powerful image we have: Isaiah's suffering servant who is, in fact, God.

Sixteenth Sunday of Ordinary Time
Year B • Mark 6:30–34

When the apostles returned to Jesus to report on their ministerial experiences on the road, he told them to come to an out-of-the-way place by themselves where they could rest. So they left by boat to such a place. But when they arrived, they found that many people who had seen them leave had arrived before them. They seemed like sheep without a shepherd. When Jesus saw them, he was moved with compassion and began to teach them at great length. After all, it was for such people that he had come in the first place. You and I are such people—or are we? Do we realize how much we need him? Our cross, in fact anything that helps us come to this realization, is a precious gift.

Monday of the Sixteenth Week
of Ordinary Time • Matthew 12:38–42

Some scribes and Pharisees asked Jesus for a sign. He answered, "An evil and unfaithful generation seeks a sign, but no sign will be given it except the sign of Jonah the prophet. Just as Jonah was in the belly of the whale three days and three nights, so will the Son of Man be in the heart of the earth three days and three nights." The Jews of the time were not concerned with accuracy about time the way we are. Jesus died on a Friday and rose on the following Sunday. That was close enough.

What is significant here is that in testing Jesus, the Pharisees were actually testing almighty God. But their real fault is not to be found in their ignorance, but in their self-centeredness. This is often the case with us as well. While the three days meant nothing to them, we have the gift of hindsight and faith. But do we also look to him with gratitude and love?

Tuesday of the Sixteenth Week
of Ordinary Time • Matthew 12:46–50

Jesus was speaking to the crowds when his Mother and brothers, or better, kinsmen, arrived outside wishing to speak to him. When notified, he stated that his mother and family are those who do the will of his heavenly Father. This was in no way a slight to his Mother, as some have inferred. On the contrary, it was an honor bestowed on those who, like her, put God first.

Throughout his public life, Jesus stressed the necessity of doing the will of his heavenly Father. But how, one may ask, can we always be sure of what that will is? So long as we strive to do it as we understand it, it is enough. Throughout her life Jesus' Mother learned the Father's will in the face of uncertainty. Since she was centered on him she learned his will—usually after she had acted. So we're in good company. We're family.

Feast of St. James, Apostle

Wednesday of the Sixteenth Week
of Ordinary Time • Matthew 20:20–28

The mother of James and John approached Jesus with the request that her two sons sit one at his right and the other at his left in his kingdom. The other disciples, upon hearing the request and fearing that they might be missing out, became indignant with them. Jesus then assured them all that, unlike the Gentiles, greatness for them had to consist of service to each other rather than in self-seeking.

Isn't this the very core of the Christian message? And yet so immersed are we in ourselves that without the help of the Lord's grace there is no way that we can get out of our own heads and act unselfishly. It is on the cross that Jesus shows us how. It is from the cross that we are empowered to do it. Incidentally, by the way the apostles turned out, there is definitely hope for us.

Thursday of the Sixteenth Week
of Ordinary Time • Matthew 13:10–17

The disciples asked Jesus, "Why do you speak to the crowd in parables?" He replied, "Because knowledge of the mysteries of the Kingdom of heaven has been granted to you, but to them it has not been granted." This is why he spoke to them in parables, because they looked but did not see and heard but did not listen or understand. They were simply not capable of absorbing all that he had to say. So he gave them what they could understand.

So with us, he gives us what we can understand and need for the moment. This is probably why he doesn't tell us the future—and also why there is so much mystery in our lives. We are just not capable of understanding the whole picture now. Besides, the act of trusting him about what we don't understand does us much good. It's provides us with another means of showing our love for him.

JULY 27, 2012

Friday of the Sixteenth Week
of Ordinary Time • Matthew 13:18–23

Jesus reveals the parable of the sower to his disciples:
The seed sown on the path is the one who hears the
word of the kingdom without understanding it. The
evil one comes and steals what is sown in the heart.
The seed sown on rocky ground is the one who hears
the word and receives it with joy but has no roots and
falls away with the first tribulation that comes along.
The seed sown on thorns is the one who hears the
word, but anxiety and the lure of riches chokes it. The
seed sown on rich soil is the one who hears the word
and understands it and bears much fruit.

So why doesn't he sow seed only on good soil and
always reap a great harvest? Well, he actually sows
the seed many times in our lifetime. Through the
suffering we endure, we are able to grow in virtue and
eventually reap the harvest. It is all calculated to help
us grow in our love for him.

Saturday of the Sixteenth Week
of Ordinary Time • Matthew 13:24–30

Jesus related a parable concerning a man who had planted wheat in his field, only to have an enemy come and sow weeds in the same field. When the wheat came up with weeds mixed in, the workers informed the man of the situation. He decided to wait until harvest to separate the weeds from the wheat, when all the plants were mature. This way there would be less chance of pulling up the wheat along with the weeds. Jesus was actually speaking of the presence of evil in the world. But he doesn't allow the wicked to live in the world along with the virtuous for fear of destroying the virtuous along with the wicked. He can tell the difference. He allows the wicked to stay around because they may become virtuous before they die. He actually suffered greatly that this might in fact happen—and it has in many instances. So you and I still have time.

Seventeenth Sunday of Ordinary Time
Year B • John 6:1–15

When Jesus came to the shore of Tiberias, a vast crowd followed him. The apostles were at a loss how to feed so many people. But with five barley loaves and a couple of dried fish, Jesus fed over five thousand with 12 full baskets left over. Jesus quickly fled to the mountains alone before the people proclaimed him king—so impressed were they at such a miracle.

Free food in their stomachs they readily understood as desirable. But eating the bread of life and drinking the cup of salvation they were in no way ready for—even though they are symbolized in the miracle Jesus performed. Two thousand years later, he feeds us with himself in a no less miraculous way that defies human understanding. It is only by faith that we know it. But nothing on earth is capable of giving such consolation and hope.

Monday of the Seventeenth Week
of Ordinary Time • Matthew 13:31–35

Jesus likened the kingdom of God to a mustard seed which, though tiny, becomes one of the largest plants when fully grown. Similarly, he likened it to yeast, which, when mixed with flour, causes it to expand greatly. So the kingdom of God is expansive. What about it?

Well, this isn't just any kingdom. He is speaking of the kingdom of God. That such a kingdom seemed insignificant to them at that time did not change the fact that it is divine in origin. With the exception of John, it was to bring them martyrdom in the wake of the news of salvation for the human race, which enables all of us to live a life of divine dimensions. This means that you and I are destined for a transformation that will make nuclear fission seem like child's play—if we are faithful!

Tuesday of the Seventeenth Week
of Ordinary Time • Matthew 13:36–43

The disciples wanted Jesus to explain to them the parable of the weeds in the field. So he told them that the Son of Man sows good seed in the field of the world. These are actually the children of the kingdom. The devil is the enemy who sows the weeds that are his children. At harvest time the Son of Man will send his angels, who will throw the weeds into the fire—while the righteous will shine like the sun in the kingdom with their Father.

During this week and next we celebrate three great founders whose followers have given themselves to saving the good seed from the bad: St. Ignatius of Loyola, St. Alphonsus Liguori, and St. Dominic. They give evidence that the weeds are still with us, but so is the Son who gives help to all who call upon him.

Wednesday of the Seventeenth Week
of Ordinary Time • Matthew 13:44–46

Jesus likened the reign of God to a buried treasure that a man found in a field. He hid it and, rejoicing, went and sold all he had and bought the field. He further likened the reign of God to a merchant's search for fine pearls. When he found a particularly valuable pearl, he sold all that he had and bought it. Jesus was speaking about the kingdom in regard to values. Values! What do we value most?

For some, getting one's way and having control is worth more than fame and wealth. But if one holds such values higher than the kingdom, then they are just as deadly as anything else that excludes God. To value the crosses in our lives is to value his cross and his love for us. Now there is real value! There is the kingdom.

Thursday of the Seventeenth Week
of Ordinary Time • Matthew 13:47–53

Jesus told the crowds that the reign of God is like a dragnet thrown into a lake, which collected all sorts of things. What was valuable was retained and what was not was thrown away. He makes the same point with several parables in which the good and bad are found together and eventually must be separated. This is by God's design.

Often people will ask why a good God allows evil. I once had a Peanuts calendar in which Lucy asked, "Why does life have to have ups and downs? Why can't it just have ups and ups and ups?" The short answer to that is that we end up loving more when we have to contend with downs. Granted, life is messier with evil, but God only allows it that a greater good may come of it. And we have to trust him on this!

Friday of the Seventeenth Week
of Ordinary Time • Matthew 13:54–58

Jesus came to his native place and taught in the local synagogue. At first the people were impressed with his wisdom but then dismissed him because of their familiarity with his family. Why is it that we say that familiarity breeds contempt? Too often we think we understand the familiar far more than we do and then make erroneous judgments as a result. Yet at the same time we loathe being misjudged ourselves.

We need to remember that respect means looking twice. We need to look twice at each other and many more times besides. It is only when we respect each other in this way that we finally behold each other. When we finally behold each other, we find we cherish each other as well. After all, this is what we were designed for.

Saturday of the Seventeenth Week
of Ordinary Time • Matthew 14:1–12

Herod, the tetrarch, had become aware of Jesus' reputation and thought that he was John the Baptist risen from the dead. He knew John to be a just man and concluded that this was the reason for his miraculous powers. Actually, he still felt guilty for putting John to death. John had angered his sister-in-law, Herodius, because he told them they shouldn't be living together. When he promised to give her daughter whatever she asked for, she told her daughter to ask for John's head. So even though so much time has passed, John still had power over him because he harbored guilt.

There was, of course, a way out for Herod. It's called repentance, and it is what John had preached. But Herod was a proud man. If there is anything in our lives that merits repentance, may we waste no time in seeking the Lord's forgiveness.

Eighteenth Sunday of Ordinary Time
Year B • John 6:24–35

When the crowd that Jesus had fed miraculously with bread and fish noticed that he was gone, they hastened to find him. When they finally found him, Jesus commented that they sought him out not because of the spiritual phenomena that they witnessed but because he had filled their stomachs. He told them that they ought to be seeking spiritual food. When he spoke of God's bread coming down from heaven, as in the case of the manna their ancestors ate, they asked for such bread. Jesus then explained, "I am the bread of life. No one who comes to me shall ever be hungry; no one who believes in me shall thirst again."

He was telling them that he actually was going to feed them with himself. He wasn't waxing poetic. He who entered our humanity was to enter our very persons—our bodies as well as our souls, transforming us into new creations.

Feast of the Transfiguration of the Lord

Monday of the Eighteenth Week
of Ordinary Time • Mark 9:2–10

Jesus took Peter, James, and John up a mountain to pray. As Jesus began to pray, his face changed in appearance, and his clothes became bright white. Moses and Elijah appeared with him, conversing about his mission. Peter offered to build three tents for them there. But as he was speaking, the voice of the Father came from a cloud above: "This is my chosen Son; listen to him." Then all became as it was. The apostles fell silent and kept the experience to themselves.

All this is in stark contrast to the garden of Gethsemane, where Jesus is seen in utter human abasement. But it is in the context of the Transfiguration that we begin to understand Gethsemane and the divine embrace that is Good Friday.

Tuesday of the Eighteenth Week
of Ordinary Time • Matthew 14:22–36

When the disciples, on a storm-tossed boat, saw Jesus walking toward them on the water, they were fearful. When Jesus calmed them, Peter asked to join him on the water and Jesus called him forth. But when Peter felt the force of the wind, he began to sink. Jesus reached out and caught him and said, "Oh you of little faith, why did you doubt?"

Peter made the great mistake of taking his eyes off Jesus. Once he centered on the storm, he forgot to trust and began to sink. How often has that happened to us—only without the water? You know what I mean: those times when our own agendas become more important to us than him! We begin to sink. He has told us in Scripture, "Without me you can do nothing!" The rejoinder to this is that without him, why would we ever want to do anything!

Wednesday of the Eighteenth Week
of Ordinary Time • Matthew 15:21–28

When a Canaanite woman asked Jesus to heal her daughter, he informed her that he was sent only to the lost sheep of Israel. She then did him homage and said, "Lord, help me." He replied, "It is not right to take the food of children and throw it to the dogs." She responded that even the dogs eat the scraps from the table. He couldn't resist such humility and replied, "Woman, great is your faith! Let it be done for you as you wish." Her daughter was healed immediately.

Humility is the key to his Sacred Heart. When we approach him with humility and faith, we are not full of ourselves. What we usually don't realize is that we are already filled with him! The virtues of humility and faith are gifts we receive from none other than him. It is the crosses that he puts in our lives that give us the opportunity to grow in such virtues.

AUGUST 10, 2012

Feast of St. Lawrence, Deacon

Friday of the Eighteenth Week
of Ordinary Time • John 12:24–26

Jesus said, "Unless a grain of wheat falls to the ground and dies, it remains a grain of wheat. But if it dies, it produces much fruit." Certainly, he was aware that the seed only appears to die. But his point was that we need to die in order to live. We are to die daily, in the sense of denying ourselves, in order to love. This is what he meant when he said that to be his followers, we need to take up our cross and follow him.

This is not a strategy that Hollywood or Madison Avenue or even most governments can fathom. Our culture goes for the easy, convenient, immediate results that gratify me first. But for those who believe, the greatest moment creation has ever known was the moment when God himself endured death that we might live as we have never lived. It remains for us to live not for ourselves but for him.

Saturday of the Eighteenth Week
of the Year • Matthew 17:14–20

A man asked Jesus to take pity on his son, who was suffering from an unclean spirit. Jesus drove the demon out and the boy was fine. His disciples asked later why they were not able to drive it out. He answered that it was because their faith was so weak. He told them that if they had faith the size of a mustard seed, they could tell a mountain to move and it would. But, of course, such faith requires a deep, personal relationship with God. Many sincere, naïve people have made extraordinary demands in the name of faith with no results. Trusting in God requires that we give him reason to trust in us. When we love someone, we don't turn the person into a means of achieving things. We ask favors of such a person only in the context of the loving relationship that binds us. So with us and God: Context is everything!

Nineteenth Sunday of Ordinary Time
Year B • John 6:41–51

The people began to murmur in protest over Jesus' claim to be the bread of life. Since they knew his family, they could not accept the claim that he had come down from heaven. "Stop your murmuring," Jesus said. "No one can come to me unless the Father who sent me draws him." He emphasizes his connection with the Father who had sent manna to their ancestors. This time the Father had sent him to give them bread that is far more life-giving than manna. Jesus affirmed that he is the living bread. "If anyone eats this bread, he shall live forever; the bread I will give is my flesh, for the life of the world."

One wonders what value there would be in eating such bread if it were only a symbol. Why would he put so much energy into a metaphor and risk losing so many of them—which he, in fact, did? It only makes sense if he meant it literally.

And oh, what a glorious mystery it truly is!

Monday of the Nineteenth Week
of Ordinary Time • Matthew 17:22–27

Jesus and his disciples met in Galilee, where he told them that he was going to be delivered into the hands of men who would put him to death, and that he would be raised up on the third day. At these words, they were overcome with grief. They then entered Capernaum, where he paid the temple tax with a coin found in the mouth of a fish. Certainly Jesus was quite capable of dealing with civil authorities and their requirements. He only became victim to their harsh judgments when he allowed it to happen.

We, on the other hand, tend to be like his disciples. When things look bleak, we want to throw in the towel. Suffering and death challenge our trust in his love for us. It remains for us to remember the blood that he shed for us and to renew our faith in him. He is so worthy of our trust!

Tuesday of the Nineteenth Week
of Ordinary Time • Matthew 18:1–5, 10, 12–14

When the disciples asked Jesus who the greatest in the kingdom of heaven were, he placed a child in their midst and said, "Unless you turn and become like little children, you will not enter the Kingdom of heaven. . . . Whoever becomes humble like this little child is the greatest in the Kingdom of heaven." In our culture, humility is often only something to be feigned, certainly not sought. It is fame and fortune that the proud seek.

So to be humiliated is to have one's pride confounded in the face of limitations that one loathes and resists. To be humbled, on the other hand, is to be a realist who honestly recognizes his limitations and readily accepts them. It is the humble person who has God's ear and can converse with him. It is only the humble who can know his friendship.

Solemnity of the Assumption of Mary

Wednesday of the Nineteenth Week
of Ordinary Time • Luke 1:39–56

When Mary visited her relative Elizabeth, her baby leapt in her womb at the approach of Mary and the nearness of his salvation in her womb. Elizabeth acknowledged Mary as the Mother of her Lord. Responding with her "Magnificat," Mary said that there is no reason to congratulate her, since it is all the work of the Lord. Her good fortune lies in the fact that God has noticed one as small as she. God is gracious, especially to the lowly and the poor.

It is through such humility that God sends his Son into the world. Today we celebrate the return of this lowly servant to her God. In celebrating the bodily Assumption of Mary into heaven, the Church acknowledges the sacredness of her mission in giving birth to the Savior and God's determination that she be so blessed. From her conception to her Assumption, Mary's life was a continuous reflection of his glory. No wonder we love her so!

Thursday of the Nineteenth Week
of Ordinary Time • Matthew 18:21–19:1

Peter asked Jesus, "Lord, if my brother sins against me, how often must I forgive him; as many as seven times?" Jesus responded, "Not seven times, but seventy-seven times." He then likened the kingdom of heaven to a king who forgave the debt of a servant. That same servant then refused to forgive the debt of one of his fellow servants. When the king heard of this, he demanded payment from the servant to whom he had given mercy. Jesus reminded them that his Father will do the same to us if we don't forgive each other from our hearts.

I'll bet you've heard this passage many times. Have you ever forgiven the same person 77 times? How about seven times? Nor have I. But we've certainly asked the Lord's forgiveness that many times and more. All the more reason to forgive each other.

Friday of the Nineteenth Week
of Ordinary Time • Matthew 19:3–12

Some Pharisees asked Jesus if it was lawful for a man to divorce his wife for any cause whatever. Jesus responded by quoting Scripture—that a man is to leave father and mother and be joined to his wife. And the two shall become one flesh. They are no longer two, but one. So they asked why Moses allowed divorce. Jesus said, "Because of the hardness of your hearts Moses allowed you to divorce your wives, but from the beginning it was not so. I say to you, whoever divorces his wife (unless the marriage is unlawful) commits adultery."

When my father died several years ago I realized how much I had related to my parents through their relationship to each other. It was tangible and alive. Now I recognize this as the presence of Jesus holding them together. Mere creatures can never remove such a presence from their lives.

Saturday of the Nineteenth Week
of Ordinary Time • Matthew 19:13–15

Parents brought their children to Jesus so that he could lay his hands on them in prayer. But the disciples scolded them for bothering Jesus. When Jesus noticed this, he said, "Let the children come to me. Do not hinder them. The kingdom of God belongs to such as these." And he drew them to himself. He knew better than anyone how pure their innocence was. This is how all his people start out. It is just such purity that he later holds up as an ideal for all of us. It takes on even greater value when chosen in the face of temptation.

Today many look down on such innocence as if it were a weakness. It is far easier to deride it than to embrace it. True heroism comes from the inside. The saints are the true heroes of humanity. They had the opportunity to serve themselves and chose to submit to him instead.

Twentieth Sunday of Ordinary Time
Year B • John 6:51–58

Jesus, knowing full well the reaction he would get, quite bluntly and emphatically states, "I myself am the living bread come down from heaven. If anyone eats this bread he shall live forever; the bread I will give is my flesh for the life of the world." The people asked how he could give them his flesh to eat, to which he replied, "Amen, amen, I say to you, unless you eat the flesh of the Son of Man and drink his blood, you do not have life within you. . . . For my flesh is real food and my blood real drink." Despite their negative reaction, he softened nothing. He knew full well the scandal that the cross would be to many of them—and the Eucharist is all about his Passion. The Passion blatantly contradicts the expectations of all who would see him in purely human terms and not in divine ones—and it still does. That God would love us that much is too much of a stretch for human sensibilities—without the help of God's grace.

AUGUST 20, 2012

Monday of the Twentieth Week
of Ordinary Time • Matthew 19:16–22

When a young man asked Jesus what good he must do to gain eternal life, Jesus told him to keep the commandments. The young man responded that he had observed all of them. He then pushed the matter further by asking what he still lacked. Jesus said to him, "If you wish to be perfect, go sell what you have and give it to the poor and you will have treasure in heaven. Then come, follow me." The young man was downcast because he had many possessions.

What possession do you have that threatens to compromise the giving of yourself unconditionally to him? It's helpful to remember that no matter what good it is, he is the source of every good. No matter what good appeals to us, it is only appealing because he is its source. Why not choose him directly so that our desire goes beyond gratifying ourselves and becomes an act of love?

Wednesday of the Twentieth Week
of Ordinary Time • Matthew 20:1–16

Jesus told his disciples the parable of the landowner who hired laborers at various times of the day but paid them all the same wage. When those who had been hired in the morning complained about being paid the same wage as those hired at the end of the day, the owner held his ground. He had paid each the amount agreed upon. If he chose to be more generous with some than others, it was his money to do with as he pleased.

My grandmother understood this. When she and her children noticed someone coming late to Mass, she would whisper, "Those who were hired at the end of the day were paid the same as the rest." Unfortunately, we aren't always as accepting of God's generosity and too often let resentment rule. We need to recognize how generous the Lord is to us. Gratitude casts out resentment.

Thursday of the Twentieth Week
of Ordinary Time • Matthew 22:1–14

Jesus likened the kingdom of God to a king who gave a wedding feast for his son and sent his servants to summon the invited guests. But they refused to come. Eventually he had them bring in strangers from the streets. Jesus was speaking of the Lord's chosen people, who refused to accept his Son.

Sometimes the more we are given, the less we appreciate generosity. How many days go by that we don't even think of thanking him for giving us the ability to know him? Simply to acknowledge who his is and to completely submit ourselves to him each day is to fulfill his purpose in giving us that day. We owe him such honesty and gratitude. The more we do this, the more we appreciate how appropriate such acknowledgment is—and the better we begin to know ourselves.

Feast of St. Bartholomew, Apostle

Friday of the Twentieth Week
of Ordinary Time • John 1:45–51

When Philip spoke of Jesus of Nazareth, Nathaniel replied, "Can anything good come from Nazareth?" Eventually, when he met Jesus, Jesus showed him that he knew him. "Before Philip called you, I saw you under the fig tree," he said. Nathaniel was quite taken that Jesus had previous knowledge of him. Jesus assured him that he would experience far greater things in the future—which he eventually did.

Like Nathaniel, we all like to be understood. Just as Jesus knew him inside as well as out, so he knows you and me in the same way. He is aware of us at this very moment. Too often we search for far lesser forms of recognition, when all the while we already have the only one that really matters.

Saturday of the Twentieth Week
of Ordinary Time • Matthew 23:1–12

Jesus exclaimed that whoever exalts himself will be humbled, but whoever humbles himself will be exalted. He spoke of the valid role the Pharisees held as teachers of the Law but warned us not to imitate their behavior. Their words were bold, but their good deeds were few. They reveled in the signs of honor they received and the titles of respect, such as "rabbi," which means teacher. They were to avoid being called teacher. Then to emphasize this, he said to call no one on earth "Father." Only God is our true father. His point was not with the terms themselves but was about not seeking earthly honors. Certainly he didn't expect people to refer to their "mother's husbands" and their "male parents" or their teachers as their "implanters of knowledge." Without understanding the context of scriptural passages, it is impossible to understand Scripture at all.

Twenty-First Sunday of Ordinary Time
Year B • John 6:60–69

Many disciples grumbled to each other about the Eucharist. "This sort of talk is hard to endure! How can anyone take it seriously?" Jesus said, "Does this shake your faith? What then if you were to see the Son of Man ascend to where he was before?" When he asked the Twelve if they would also go away, Peter, typically, spoke for the rest and answered, "Lord, to whom shall we go? You have the words of eternal life. We have come to believe; we are convinced that you are God's holy one." There was simply no way they could understand his words without faith.

Since the 16th century even some Christians have tried reducing the Eucharist to only a symbol. Others have placed the eucharistic Presence in the mind of the believer. Both of these feeble attempts do no justice to the mystery of the Eucharist, which is really the mystery of the Passion. The apostles came to believe because they loved him. Enough said!

Monday of the Twenty-First Week
of Ordinary Time • Matthew 23:13–22

Jesus said, "Woe to you scribes and Pharisees, you hypocrites. You traverse sea and land to make one convert, and when that happens you make him a child of Gehenna twice as much as yourselves. . . . And you say, 'If one swears by the altar, it means nothing, but if one swears by the gift on the altar, one is obligated.' You blind ones, which is greater, the gift, or the altar that makes the gift sacred?"

What the scribes and Pharisees were doing was reprehensible to our Blessed Lord. By their dishonesty they were duping his people—and in the name of God, no less! Nothing angered Jesus more than pretense and dishonesty—but especially at the expense of the lowly who recognize their lowliness. He only came for the lowly. Get it?

Tuesday of the Twenty–First Week
of Ordinary Time • Matthew 23:23–26

Jesus bellowed, "Woe to you scribes and Pharisees, you frauds! You pay tithes on mint and herbs and seeds while neglecting the weightier matters of the law: justice and mercy and good faith. It is these you should have practiced, without neglecting the others. Blind guides!" While the scribes and Pharisees often found fault with Jesus, they could never convict him of any wrongdoing. But they tried very hard to reduce his credibility with others, especially the simple. This infuriated him. Their own blindness disconcerted him, but it was their wayward influence on the innocent that enraged him. And this is still the case. We are all called to lift the spirits of the innocent, not to scandalize them with dishonest words or bad example. People notice our actions far more than we realize. The next generation is watching our behavior. Are we?

Memorial of the Beheading of John the Baptist

Wednesday of the Twenty-First Week
of Ordinary Time • Mark 6:17–29

During a gala birthday banquet, the daughter of Herod's sister-in-law-turned-wife, Herodius, performed a dance that greatly pleased him. He promised to give her whatever she asked for. Her mother told her to ask for the head of John the Baptist. The king was deeply distressed over this, for he respected John, but he had made a promise.

So John's life was terminated over a mere trifle. His death was a reminder to Jesus that the preparation for his coming was past, his own death was drawing near—a death no less senseless—and yet the event that was to eclipse the grandeur of the very creation of all that is, a death that means eternal life for you and me.

Thursday of the Twenty-First Week
of Ordinary Time • Matthew 24:42–51

Jesus said to his disciples, "Stay awake! For you do not know on which day the Lord will come. You can be sure that if the master of the house had known the hour of night when the thief was coming, he would have stayed awake and not let his house be broken into. So you too, must be prepared, or at an hour you do not expect, the Son of man will come."

We see Jesus' concerns about their being prepared for the unexpected borne out when he was arrested. When he ordered the apostles to cease reacting with violence, they became frantic and fled. So with us, who of us is beyond losing our perspective in the face of trials, especially severe trials? All the more reason to stay focused on the crucifix and the divine love we find there. Truly there is our salvation!

Saturday of the Twenty-First Week of Ordinary Time • Matthew 25:14–30

Jesus told a parable in which a man, before leaving on journey, handed five thousand silver pieces to one servant, to a second, two thousand, and to a third, one thousand. When he returned, the first had doubled the five thousand by investing it. The second doubled the two thousand he had received. The third, however, buried his one thousand for safety. The man rewarded the first two and punished the third for not at least banking the money for interest and for his rationalizations and laziness.

We were meant for more than living with our brakes on. It is amazing what energy we can muster when we are committed to something or someone. As Jesus hung on the cross, his upstretched arms squeezed his lungs. So he had to push down on his crucified feet to raise his body in order to breathe. Giving his all, he managed to do this over and over for three hours, until he had no strength left. No one has ever loved you so much!

Twenty-Second Sunday of Ordinary Time
Year B • Mark 7:1–8, 14–15, 21–23

Some Pharisees asked Jesus why his disciples ignored their ancestral traditions by eating food without washing their hands. He responded by quoting the prophet Isaiah. "This people pay me lip service, but their heart is far from me. Empty is the reverence they do me because they teach as dogmas mere human precepts." He told the crowd that nothing from outside the person can make one impure. Only things such as acts of fornication, theft, murder, adulterous conduct, greed, arrogance, and the like, which come from within the human heart, can make one impure. So it is what we know and choose that determines the morality of our actions—not the mere appearance of them.

When they wanted to stone a woman for adultery, Jesus saw her remorse and contrition while the crowd only saw a woman caught in the act of sin. How fortunate we are that we have him as the judge of our souls for all eternity.

Monday of the Twenty-Second Week
of Ordinary Time • Luke 4:16–30

In his native synagogue, Jesus read aloud the scriptural passage, "The Spirit of the Lord is upon me because he has anointed me to bring glad tidings to the poor." He then acknowledged that the passage was about him. At first they were amazed, but then they became skeptical. He told them that no prophet was ever welcome in his native place. Highly insulted, the people tried to throw him down a cliff, but he escaped.

Have you ever reflected that one is never humbly insulted? Have we ever seen people fight out of righteous humility? "It was humility that drove him to such resentment!" I think you catch my drift. It was pride that kept those people from recognizing who Jesus was. The same can happen to us. I like the bumper sticker I saw one day that read, "Too blessed to be oppressed." Isn't that the truth!

Tuesday of the Twenty-Second Week
of Ordinary Time • Luke 4:31–37

When a man with an unclean spirit approached Jesus in the synagogue, he rebuked the spirit, which then left the man. The people were amazed. "What is there about his words? For with authority and power he commands the unclean spirits and they come out." News about him spread everywhere in the surrounding region.

We live in a culture that distrusts authority while at the same time admiring what is authoritative. Actually, to speak with authority is to speak with fidelity to the author, that is, the one the speaker represents. In the case of our Lord, he was representing the Father, who is the Author of all and from whom all lawful authority comes. *Obedience* comes from the Latin *ab audire*, "to hear." It remains for us to obey lawful authority because in doing so we are allowing ourselves to hear the Author, the Lord God, himself.

Thursday of the Twenty-Second Week
of Ordinary Time • Luke 5:1–11

After preaching to the people from the boat, Jesus had Peter set out to the deeper waters for a catch. Peter obeyed despite having caught nothing all night. When he complied, they caught so much fish that the boats were on the verge of sinking. Clearly more was happening than the purely natural—and Peter no longer addressed Jesus as Master but as Lord. "Depart from me, Lord, for I am a sinful man." Jesus responded, "Do not be afraid. From now on you will be catching men." With that the apostles brought their boats to land, left everything, and followed him.

So Peter followed him by acknowledging his sinfulness and submitting to him. The others followed suit. It is always this way. To become his follower is to humbly submit oneself to him and his superior judgment.

Friday of the Twenty-Second Week
of Ordinary Time • Luke 5:33–39

The scribes and Pharisees complained that the disciples of Jesus didn't fast and pray as did their disciples and those of the Baptist. Jesus responded that the wedding guests didn't fast as long as the bridegroom was with them—inferring that as long as he was with them they were not to fast. The day would come when he would be taken from them and then they would fast. There is an appropriate time for feasting and an appropriate time for fasting.

So with his Church, there are times for feasting and for fasting, and they are determined by what part of his life the Church is directing us to give attention to. From the "Lord have mercies" of Lent to the "alleluias" of Easter, our lives are all about his.

Feast of the Birth of Mary

Saturday of the Twenty-Second Week
of Ordinary Time • Matthew 1:1–16, 18–23

We have a genealogy that ends with Joseph and avoids any mention of his begetting Jesus. Joseph offers legal paternity, but it is Mary, his betrothed, who begot Jesus. Joseph was the intimate guardian, teacher, and observer. The parent, in the fullest sense, is Mary, whose true spouse is God, the Holy Spirit. No other human being has ever been so honored. To say that Catholics over-honor her is to disregard the reality of her divine espousal and parenthood. The Triune God has honored her far beyond anything Catholics can do.

Nevertheless, we do honor her—precisely because of God's direct and unique intervention in her life. Such honor is in response to his deliberate choice and is a mere echo of it. Today we honor the birth of this very special woman. Holy Mary, Mother of God, pray for us sinners now and at the hour of our death.

Twenty-Third Sunday of Ordinary Time
Year B • Mark 7:31–37

Some people brought a deaf man to Jesus and begged him to lay his hands on him. Jesus then took the man away from the crowd, put his finger in the man's ears, and spitting, touched the man's tongue. He then addressed the man's ears and tongue, saying, "Be opened!" Immediately the man was healed. Jesus told him to tell no one, but of course, in his excitement, he told everyone he met. Those who witnessed this were highly impressed.

Certainly we would have been impressed also. In fact, we would have been ecstatic! But the fact is, most of us have been able to hear and speak all our lives. Why are we not ecstatic? We seldom appreciate what we have always had. But most of all, we forget how generous the Lord is with us, don't we? The same love that healed that man has been with us all our lives. We would do well to spend the rest of our lives thanking him.

Monday of the Twenty-Third Week
of Ordinary Time • Luke 6:6–11

When confronted with a man's withered hand on the Sabbath, Jesus asked the scribes and Pharisees, "Is it lawful to do good on the Sabbath—or evil; to preserve life—or to destroy it?" He looked at them and then told the man to stretch out his hand, which he healed on the spot. The scribes and Pharisees were aghast. Fully aware that Sabbath observance was never meant to come before charity, Jesus cut through their petty concerns by putting first things first. It was his familiarity with the will of the Author that caused so many people to praise him for speaking with authority.

Through his Church he speaks today with the same authority, giving priority to life over personal choice, marriage until death over divorce, sexual purity over lust and sexual aberrations. To get your priorities right is to live the truth!

Tuesday of the Twenty-Third Week
of Ordinary Time • Luke 6:12–19

Jesus went to a mountain to pray, spending the night in communion with his Father. At daybreak he selected 12 disciples to be his apostles. Mentioning Simon Peter first, the Gospel is clear that his choices were specific and deliberate. Coming down the mountain with them, he exposed them to a large crowd of people. He deliberately went from a night of prayer to handpicking apostles to immersing them in the crowds who needed them. Note that he preceded all important events with prayer and fasting. This is how the Church came about and it is how it continues.

How many times did we see Pope John Paul praying everywhere, on planes, in chapels, or standing and leaning his head against the crucifix on his staff? Prayer is a matter of speaking from the heart and listening as well. Often there are no words; it's just letting the soul breathe.

Thursday of the Twenty-Third Week
of Ordinary Time • Luke 6:27–38

Jesus exhorted his disciples to meet persecution with charity alone. "Love your enemies," he said. "Do good to those who hate you, bless those who curse you, pray for those who mistreat you." He warns against the temptation to judge one's self better than others. Make others better by your good example, even correcting them when necessary. But begin with yourself. Only the good can do good.

This sounds fine, but who can really do it? All a person has to do is cut in front of us on the highway or in line in the grocery store and we want to eat them alive. The apostles were no different from us—yet most of them ended by giving their lives for the benefit of others. When in humility we recognize our complete dependence on him to love just a little, he will give us the same strength he gave them. The question is: How much do we really want it?

Feast of the Triumph of the Cross

Friday of the Twenty-Third Week
of Ordinary Time • John 3:13–17

Jesus said to Nicodemus, "Just as Moses lifted up the serpent in the desert, so must the Son of Man be lifted up, so that everyone who believes in him may have eternal life." He was speaking, of course, about his Crucifixion.

When one considers all the various means of capital punishment that have existed throughout history, none of us would ever dream of exalting or paying homage to them. Yet we hold the cross so dear that we Catholics even sign ourselves with it. Given the fact that we revere Jesus who suffered so as the result of it, why do we not disdain the cross? It is his love that makes the difference. It is his presence on the cross that transforms it. Today we exalt because we exult. We exalt—we hold up this instrument of death, because we exult—we rejoice in Jesus who is our life!

Memorial of Our Lady of Sorrows

Saturday of the Twenty-Third Week
of Ordinary Time • John 19:25–27

Jesus looked down from the cross on his Mother and
the apostle John and said, "Woman, behold your son,"
and to John he said, "Behold your mother." From that
hour the disciple took her to his home. Certainly, if
Mary had other children he would not have given her
to the care of John. She had no one but him. Evidently
Joseph had already died.

But Jesus had more in mind than simply her care.
He was thinking of us. John's mother was living and
was actually present also. But sacred Tradition tells us
that in giving his Mother to John, Jesus was giving her
to the whole world—which completed his total gift to
us. Besides his own life, she was the most precious
gift he had to give and he held nothing back. Besides
his suffering, no one suffered as much as she did that
day. She remains a model of fidelity and love for every
Christian. But most of all, she is our Mother.

Twenty-Fourth Sunday of Ordinary Time
Year B • Mark 8:27–35

Jesus asked his disciples who people said that he was. After they mentioned some prophets and others, he said, "And you, who do you say that I am?" Peter, speaking for the rest, answered, "You are the Messiah!" Jesus ordered them not to tell this to anyone. He then told them that he would have to suffer much, be rejected by the elders, chief priests, and scribes and be put to death—and rise three days later. Peter tried to convince him that this should not happen. Jesus responded, "Get out of my sight, you Satan. You are not judging by God's standards but by man's."

How would you like to have Jesus refer to you as Satan? I wouldn't either. Our Lord was making it quite clear just how wrong it is to counter the Father's will. Of course, Peter didn't understand the significance of what God wanted and how good it was ultimately. We need to focus on this the next time we are baffled by whatever the Lord has put in front of us.

Monday of the Twenty-Fourth Week of Ordinary Time • Luke 7:1–10

When a centurion sent some elders to Jesus that he might heal his mortally ill servant, he complied. As he drew near, the centurion sent friends to tell him that he did not consider himself worthy to have Jesus enter his house, but just to say the word and he knew that his slave would be well. Touched by his faith and humility, Jesus remarked that not even in Israel had he encountered such faith—a faith that recognized his special relationship with the Father and the divine character of his mission, which the Jews refused to do. He healed the man immediately.

Today, the Church still recalls the centurion as she puts his words on our lips: "Lord, I am not worthy to receive you, but only say the word and I shall be healed." It remains for us to allow those words to issue from our hearts as they did from his.

SEPTEMBER 18, 2012

Tuesday of the Twenty-Fourth Week
of Ordinary Time • Luke 7:11–17

As Jesus approached a town, a dead man was being carried out, the only son of a widowed mother. Moved with pity, he said to her, "Do not cry." He stepped forward, touched the litter, and said, "Young man, I bid you get up." The dead man sat up and began to speak. Fear seized the people, who began to praise God. Notice how we react when confronted with the unknown over which we have no control? We are quite vulnerable all the time wherever we are. All kinds of things can happen to us. But our Blessed Lord is always present as well. Every beat of our hearts gives evidence of his power. And when they eventually stop, he is still in control. One day may we meet that young man and his mother after having lived a life of fidelity to the one who has always been with us.

Thursday of the Twenty-Fourth Week
of Ordinary Time • Luke 7:36–50

A Pharisee invited Jesus to dinner—not a common occurrence. A woman, known as a sinner, learned of his presence there and appeared with a vase of perfumed ointment. Bending over his feet and weeping, she bathed them with her tears and dried them with her long hair. She then anointed them with the ointment. Immediately, the Pharisee was put off by her presence and the fact that Jesus accepted her gesture. Jesus then asked him which of two men would be the most grateful for having their debts written off: the one who owed little or the one who owed much. The Pharisee responded that the one who had owed the most would be most grateful. So with sinners. "I tell you," he said, "that is why her many sins are forgiven—because she has loved much. Little is forgiven the one whose love is small." Hearing this, how could anyone fear going to confession!

Feast of St. Matthew, Apostle and Evangelist

Friday of the Twenty-Fourth Week
of Ordinary Time • Matthew 9:9–13

Matthew told Jesus that he worked as a tax collector when Jesus came by and asked him to follow him. He immediately left his post and followed him. As a tax collector, he was looked down upon by the Jews because he was working for the Romans under whom they lived in their own country. It is interesting to note that both Mark and Luke only identify him as Levi in their Gospels out of kindness to him. But in his own Gospel he readily admits of the life he had lived before Jesus called him. When a Pharisee gave a dinner for Jesus, he commented on Jesus associating with such people. Overhearing him, Jesus responded that the healthy do not need doctors; only the sick do. He came to call sinners, not the self-righteous. Isn't it a consolation that he came for the likes of you and me? There isn't a greater one.

Saturday of the Twenty-Fourth Week of Ordinary Time • Luke 8:4–15

Jesus told the parable of the farmer who sowed seed, with some falling on foot paths, on rocky ground, among briers and thorns. None of these seeds were able to grow to maturity. But some fell on good soil and did grow, yielding a hundredfold. His disciples pressed him for the parable's meaning. So he likened the seed to the word of God. Much of it falls on ears that reject it for any of several reasons. But some of it is heard by people who are open to it and act on it. It then bears fruit by their perseverance. In fact they were acting out the parable without even realizing it because they wanted to understand it. Their openness to it allowed Jesus to explain it to them, which in turn would bear fruit. It was to these men that Jesus was to entrust his Church after he left them. Today their successors teach us still. You must be rich soil since you are listening.

Twenty-Fifth Sunday of Ordinary Time
Year B • Mark 9:30–37

As Jesus and his disciples walked through Galilee, he spoke to them about the future, saying that he would be put to death and would rise in three days. Though they didn't understand what he was talking about, they were afraid to ask him. When they reached their destination, he asked them what they had been arguing about on the way. They were embarrassed to answer, but he knew that they had been arguing about which of them was the most important. He showed them that he who chooses to be last and the least is the most important, turning pride on its head.

They were afraid to deal with their fear of losing him, but by focusing on themselves, they inevitably ran into trouble. Yet he gently let it all unfold. Eventually, they would understand. How like us they were. His patience with us is equaled only by his love for us.

Monday of the Twenty-Fifth Week
of Ordinary Time • Luke 8:16–18

Jesus told the crowd that no one who lights a lamp conceals it, but rather he puts it on a stand where people may benefit from it. "There is nothing hidden," he said, "that will not become visible and nothing secret that will not become known and come to light."

He obviously was not speaking of the way one lights one's home. He was concerned with how attentive we are to him and what he has to reveal. For those who are half-hearted, what little faith they have will disappear. But to those who are earnest and truly want to know his will, to those will he reveal himself. He wants our attention at this very moment. How interested we are in him and what he wants as opposed to our own agendas will determine with just how much of his light we will be filled.

Tuesday of the Twenty-Fifth Week
of Ordinary Time • Luke 8:19–21

Jesus was told that his Mother and brothers were standing outside and wished to speak with him. Since the language had no word for "cousin," the word for "brother" was used to designate close kin in general. His mother and other relatives were unable to get close to him because of the crowd. Jesus responded with the words, "My mother and my brothers are those who hear the word of God and act on it."

Far from being a slight to his mother, his words dramatically emphasize the kind of relationship he desires from his followers. To do the will of the Father is to be family with God. Mary scores here as well. Not only is she family with God, since she is the Mother of Jesus; she is also a member of God's family because her whole life was taken up with doing the will of the Father!

Wednesday of the Twenty-Fifth Week
of Ordinary Time • Luke 9:1–6

Jesus gave the Twelve power and authority over all demons and the ability to cure diseases, and sent them to proclaim the kingdom of God and to heal the sick. He told them to take nothing for the journey, no walking stick, no sack, no food, money, or second tunic. As with so many people in training, they really had little idea of all they were truly preparing for. The day was to come for each of them when their words would be so crucial to those who heard them that they would either be received with great joy or their lives would be in jeopardy.

Like them, as we prepare for the future by our present activity, so much mystery lies before us. Jesus has called us also to follow his lead, to trust him and be faithful. With the disciples, our future lies in our fidelity to him.

Thursday of the Twenty-Fifth Week
of Ordinary Time • Luke 9:7–9

When Herod learned that Jesus was preaching in Galilee, he said, "John I beheaded. Who then is this about whom I hear such things?" He had been bothered by the truth of the Baptist's words, yet he found himself wanting to listen.

All through history there have been those who have been repulsed by the message of Jesus and his Church and yet have not been able to shake their attraction to it. We see this today so blatantly with the secular media and the entertainment industry, particularly with Hollywood. No matter how much one detests the Catholic Church, it is impossible to ignore it. It touches people at a level of such depth that they are powerless to resist. This is because every human being was created for the truth and longs for him. Day in and day out, he speaks through his Church.

Friday of the Twenty-Fifth Week
of Ordinary Time • Luke 9:18–22

When praying in solitude Jesus asked his disciples, "Who do the crowds say that I am?" They replied with John the Baptist, Elijah, or one of the early prophets. "But you," he asked, "who do you say that I am?" Peter replied, "The Christ of God."

Recently someone on our online "Ask an Apologist" forum asked when we should pray to God and when to the saints. Of course, God is first before all of his creation—even though his saints all point to him. When we look to Jesus, we look to divinity. He is like us in his humanity but almighty God in his divinity: the perfect mediator. We acknowledge this in our prayer. But we acknowledge this most by our faithfulness to him in the way we live our lives. The saints help us with this by their example and their prayers for us.

Feast of the Archangels Michael, Gabriel, and Raphael

Saturday of the Twenty-Fifth Week of Ordinary Time • John 1:47–51

When the apostle Nathaniel first met Jesus, he was overwhelmed by all that Jesus knew about him. Jesus responded that he would eventually see heaven opened and the angels of God ascending and descending on the Son of Man. Today people often tell their children that they will become angels when they go to heaven.

But we do not and cannot become angels. Angels are pure spirits and far more intelligent than we. The word *angel* means "messenger." Those who are known for extraordinary messages are called archangels, such as Michael, Gabriel, and Raphael, whom we celebrate today. We refer to them as saints because saints are those beings who dwell in heaven. The angels are at God's beck and call. Theirs is the honor of serving him directly and being fully aware of what they are doing and whom they are serving. We have to wait for heaven for such knowledge—but heaven is worth the wait!

Twenty-Sixth Sunday of Ordinary Time
Year B • Mark 9:38–43, 45, 47–48

When asked about a man who used the name of Jesus to expel demons, Jesus responded that he was not to be stopped. "Anyone who is not against us is with us," he said. Anyone who would give a person a drink of water in his name will not go without a reward. But if anyone leads another astray, it would be better that he be thrown into the sea with a millstone tied around his neck. He then emphasized the danger of falling into sin. "If your hand is your difficulty, cut it off!" he said. Certainly he wasn't encouraging people to do harm to their bodies. But cutting themselves off from him is far worse than going through life maimed or blind.

Nothing, absolutely nothing is worth committing a mortal sin—which is to betray him. He is so worth submitting our lives to. Nothing matters as much!

Monday of the Twenty-Sixth Week
of Ordinary Time • Luke 9:46–50

Responding to the disciples' desire for self-honor, Jesus said, "The one who is least among all of you is the one who is the greatest." Now doesn't that set our culture on its head! He couldn't mean that a vagrant is more important than a head of state, could he? There's no doubt that a head of state's responsibilities are greater. But what our Lord is really saying is that he values the lowly far more than the proud. We see this throughout the Gospels.

Today we also see this in the 19th century Carmelite nun Saint Therese of Lisieux. It was through the honesty of humility that she became a great saint and Doctor of the Church. Through her willingness to be insignificant and totally his, she has become one of the most renowned of all saints. Through her the Lord continued to demonstrate to us the same message that still has not sunken in for most of us.

Memorial of the Guardian Angels

Tuesday of the Twenty-Sixth Week
of Ordinary Time • Matthew 18:1–5, 10

When Jesus speaks of the innocence of children, he says, "Their angels in heaven always look upon the Father's face." He's speaking, of course, about their guardian angels.

Talk of such angels can be found in early rabbinic writings. Luke also writes of Peter's angel in Acts 12:15. Though we are seldom aware of them, they guard us from physical harm and from spiritual harm as well. Their presence is a sign of God's love for us—and for them! Since it is in their love for us and for God that they serve us, they benefit as well. Love is like that. In loving us, they grow more loving themselves—as do we when we put ourselves out for one another. We can look forward to finally meeting them in heaven and learning how much their loving concern for us has helped us to join them before the face of God.

Thursday of the Twenty-Sixth Week
of Ordinary Time • Luke 10:1–12

Jesus sent 72 disciples ahead of him in pairs to every town he was to visit. He gave them specific orders: They were to carry no money bag, no sack, and no sandals. If they were received by people in peace they were to stay with them and accept their hospitality in payment for their labors. They were to cure the sick and announce that "the Kingdom of God is at hand."

In other words, they were to serve him while putting their welfare completely in his hands. They were to relinquish control and trust him. This was to be the context in which they lived and worked. How well would you manage living your daily life in such a context? Whether you are aware of it or not, this is your context, too. How's it going? If not well, the solution is not to control more but to trust more.

Friday of the Twenty-Sixth Week
of Ordinary Time • Luke 10:13–16

When sending 72 disciples out to preach and heal, Jesus told them, "Whoever listens to you listens to me. Whoever rejects you rejects me. And whoever rejects me rejects the one who sent me." In preparing them for his future absence, he gives further evidence of his intention to found a Church and to give it authority. Today, when Peter's successor, the pope of Rome, speaks, the whole world listens. Even their resistance to his words testifies to his great influence—an influence that originates far beyond his own person.

"Whoever listens to you listens to me. Whoever rejects you rejects me." For over two thousand years his Church has made him present among us in Scripture, in sacrament, and in her authoritative teaching. He can be found nowhere else.

Saturday of the Twenty–Sixth Week
of Ordinary Time • Luke 10:17–24

When the 72 disciples returned from ministering, they rejoiced to Jesus over having had power over demons that were subject to his name. But he responded, "I watched Satan fall from the sky like lightning. . . . Do not rejoice so much in the fact that devils are subject to you as that your names are written in heaven." He then rejoiced in the Holy Spirit over his relationship with the Father. Finally, by his incarnation, the power of Satan was beginning to be overcome! Then he turned to them and said, "Blest are the eyes that see what you see." Many prophets and kings wished to see what they saw and hear what they heard and did not have that privilege.

So we have the same reason to rejoice. He has in fact overcome the power of Satan by his Passion. We see evidence of this every time we witness his body and blood on the altar and receive him into our bodies. One day we will be able to appreciate this fully and that will be heaven—really!

OCTOBER 7, 2012

Twenty-Seventh Sunday of Ordinary Time
Year B • Mark 10:2–16

In an effort to test Jesus, some Pharisees asked him if it was permissible for a husband to divorce his wife. When he asked what Moses had prescribed regarding divorce, they answered that he permitted it. Jesus responded that he permitted divorce because of the people's stubbornness, but this was not so in the beginning. He created them male and female so that a man shall leave his father and mother and the two shall become one. They are no longer two, but one flesh. Therefore no one may separate what God has joined. The one who divorces one's spouse and marries another commits adultery against that spouse. Despite the clarity of these statements of Jesus, the Catholic Church remains nearly alone today in upholding them. "What God has joined!" We live in a culture that sees religion as stifling the human personality because it mistakes license for freedom.

Tuesday of the Twenty-Seventh Week
of Ordinary Time • Luke 10:38–42

When Jesus visited some friends, one of them, named Martha, welcomed him. Her sister Mary sat before him, listening to him. Martha, burdened with much serving, complained to him that her sister had left her to do all the work and asked him to tell Mary to help her. Jesus responded, "Martha, you are anxious and worried about many things. Mary has chosen the better part and it will not be taken from her."

Note that he didn't deny the work's value, but simply suggested that listening to him was better. No matter how active we are, we all need to set aside some time to sit at his feet in silence. Just looking at a crucifix and cherishing the love we find there is prayer. It doesn't need words. Our gratitude is all he asks. A grateful person is always nice to have around—especially when that person is ourselves.

Wednesday of the Twenty-Seventh Week of Ordinary Time • Luke 11:1–4

A disciple asked Jesus, "Lord, teach us to pray as John taught his disciples." So Jesus taught him the perfect prayer—which has come to be known as the Lord's Prayer, or as Catholics like to say, the "Our Father." In Matthew's Gospel, "For thine is the Kingdom and the power and the glory for ever and ever, Amen" was added later for liturgical reasons but was not a part of the original text, as people later assumed that is was. The Church actually stopped using that last part until the liturgical reforms of Vatican II, when it reintroduced it. Many of us grew up thinking that it was the Protestant way. But it is actually a Catholic addition that predates Protestantism by quite some time.

This prayer of Jesus is usually the first prayer that Catholics learn. At the close of our lives may it also be on our lips: "But deliver us from evil, Amen."

Thursday of the Twenty-Seventh Week
of Ordinary Time • Luke 11:5–13

Jesus speaks of a man to whom a friend goes at midnight and says, "Friend, lend me three loaves of bread." The man responds that his door is locked since the household has retired for the night. Jesus adds that if he does not get up to give him the loaves out of friendship, he will because of his friend's persistence. Then he says, "Ask and you shall receive, knock and the door will be opened. For everyone who asks receives. And the one who seeks finds."

It is true that Jesus warned against babbling like the pagans. But the emphasis was on "pagans," not on repetitious prayer. In many places in Scripture, Jesus encourages us to persist with our prayer. Remember the sinner who just kept repeating, "Lord, have mercy on me, a sinner"? Jesus said that he went home justified—repetitious prayer and all.

Friday of the Twenty-Seventh Week of Ordinary Time • Luke 11:15–26

Some people said that Jesus drove out demons by the power of Beelzubul, the prince of demons. Jesus responded that every kingdom divided against itself will be laid waste. "If Satan is divided against himself, how will his kingdom stand? . . . But if it is by the finger of God that I drive them out, then the Kingdom of God has come upon you."

Just as cancer turns the body against itself when the multiplying out-of-control cells overcome the healthy ones, serious sin snuffs out virtue in the soul. This is why such sin is called mortal or deadly. Unlike cancer, mortal sin has a cure that is readily available. The cure is repentance, a firm resolve to turn away from sin and the forgiveness by our Blessed Lord in the absolution he gives through his priests. It is by the finger of God that we are forgiven and his kingdom is truly upon us.

Saturday of the Twenty-Seventh Week
of Ordinary Time • Luke 11:27–28

While Jesus was speaking, a woman in the crowd cried out, "Blessed is the womb that bore you and the breasts that nursed you!" "Rather," he replied, "blessed are they who hear the word of God and keep it." Now in no way is his reply a negation or diminishing of the unfathomable honor of bearing God in one's womb or nursing God at one's breast as his Mother did. Anyone given such an intimate and exalted role in the Incarnation and Redemption has to be very, very close to God. And this is what makes his next statement so powerful. He says that we who hear him and keep his word are related to him in such intimacy.

But what if we haven't been keeping his word and don't know how to start? Well, we start by wanting to. Love begins by willing it. Leave no stone unturned until you learn more. Check out catholic.com and ewtn.com. You are in our prayers.

Monday of the Twenty-Eighth Week of Ordinary Time • Luke 11:29–32

Jesus told the people that though their evil generation sought a sign, it would receive only the sign of Jonah. He noted that at the preaching of Jonah, the Ninevites repented, but there was something, meaning himself, greater than Jonah in their midst—but they were blind to him. Although the Ninevites sinned, they repented because they were humbled. But the evil generation are not humbled and see no reason to repent. That's the way it is with pride. It turns people completely into themselves.

How do we know that we are not filled with pride? Attempting to measure our humility only focuses us in on ourselves. But checking on how grateful we are turns our attention to the giver. Nothing humbles us more than recognizing the gift of our existence and the Savior's blood that was shed for us. At such moments we know that someone greater than Jonah is in our midst.

Tuesday of the Twenty-Eighth Week
of Ordinary Time • Luke 11:37–41

When Jesus did not observe the prescribed washing before eating, a Pharisee voiced his shock. "Oh you Pharisees," Jesus responded. "Although you cleanse the outside of the cup and dish, inside you are filled with plunder and evil. Did not the Creator of the outside of the dish also make the inside? But as to what is within, give alms, and behold, everything will be clean for you." So he encouraged them to generosity by giving alms, which would make them cleaner inside than all their many outer purifications.

Only the Lord has complete access to our interior life. Only he knows how guilty and how innocent we are, how much we love and how little. We spend so much energy on the outside when it's the inside that will determine our eternity. The Lord waits for us from within for the love we have to offer him!

Wednesday of the Twenty-Eighth Week of Ordinary Time • Luke 11:42–46

Jesus chastised the Pharisees for observing the Law's minutiae but ignoring whatever pertains directly to God. He objected to their seeking out seats of honor and public recognition. When some Law scholars stated that they felt insulted by what he said to the Pharisees, he turned on them as well because of their imposition of burdens on others that they themselves would not carry.

Nowhere do we find our Blessed Lord more irate than when he dealt with the dishonesty of the proud. Their sinfulness was not the result of weakness but of their self-serving desire for prestige and power over others. But with the sinfulness of the humble he had nothing but compassion, because they acknowledged their need for him. There is the key: to want things his way over our own. If the Pharisees had only wanted this, they would have known his compassion as well.

Feast of St. Luke, Evangelist

Thursday of the Twenty-Eighth Week
of Ordinary Time • Luke 10:1–9

Jesus sent his disciples out in pairs to preach the coming of the kingdom and told them that he was sending them out like lambs among wolves with no money bag and no sandals. From a purely human perspective they were quite vulnerable. But his perspective was much more than human. They didn't realize the power of evil that awaited them—nor the superior power of his grace at their disposal.

Luke, whom we celebrate today, was a convert whom grace completely refashioned. We all start out at zero. It is the Lord who touches us and gives us the gift of faith in his own way, and seldom do we realize the power of his presence within us. Sometimes it is only by the spiritual dangers that we have encountered and survived that we recognize the proximity of his power. His hand is on each one of us far more than we know.

Friday of the Twenty-Eighth Week
of Ordinary Time • Luke 12:1–7

Jesus warns not to be afraid of those who kill the body but of the one who after killing has the power to cast one into Gehenna. Even sparrows sold for two small coins do not escape the notice of God. "The hairs on your head are counted," he said. "Fear not; you are worth more than many sparrows."

Most of us fear rejection, the disapproval of people we respect, and certainly we fear for our physical safety. But our Blessed Lord is telling us that the only safety that ultimately matters is safety from sin and temptation. How much do we fear them? You won't find NBC or even Fox News doing a special warning of the dangers of sin. Our ultimate safety lies in repentance and the willingness to forego anything and everything in order to be faithful to him.

OCTOBER 20, 2012

Saturday of the Twenty-Eighth Week
of Ordinary Time • Luke 12:8–12

Jesus spoke to the disciples of how they are to preach and teach. He told them that whoever acknowledges him before men, he will acknowledge before God's angels, that is, before the Father. But whoever disowns him here will be disowned there. Whoever disowns him to the Father blasphemes the Holy Spirit. To deny God to God is the most hopeless thing one could do. But if one honestly repents, God will forgive him. Jesus went on to assure them that in defending him before rulers and authorities, they need not worry about what to say. The Holy Spirit would instruct them at the moment what to say.

Many times Catholics will shy away from defending their faith publicly for fear of doing it inadequately. It would help them considerably if they stopped worrying about how they appear and offered their love to the Lord and asked for help. Then God can work with whatever they say—no matter how inadequate they may think it sounds.

Twenty-Ninth Sunday of Ordinary Time
Year B • Mark 10:35–45

When Zebedee's sons, James and John, asked Jesus to let them sit at his right and at his left in the kingdom, Jesus commented that such was not his to give because it was up to the Father. When the other 10 became aware of what they had asked, they became indignant for fear of losing out. Jesus admonished them. "You know how among the Gentiles those who seem to exercise authority lord it over them; their great ones make their importance felt. It cannot be like that with you." To achieve greatness is to serve the rest. The Son of Man came to serve and to give his life as a ransom for many. Of course they didn't understand. Yet John would be the only apostle with the courage to stand at the foot of the cross and James would be the first apostle to give up his life for Jesus. The strength he gave to them he can give to you and me—if we let him.

Tuesday of the Twenty-Ninth Week
of Ordinary Time • Luke 12:35–38

Jesus told his disciples to gird their loins and light their lamps like servants awaiting their master's return. If the master returned and found them vigilant, he would proceed to wait on them! And should he come even later and found them attentive, "blessed will those servants be."

For the Church, keeping vigil has meant more than simply waiting or staying awake. Girding our loins means being ready for action. It's not a passive thing. The Lord himself told us that attention to him must come before all other concerns. Why not give him some daily time before the family is up and the day has begun? Such time is golden, and he deserves it. When he finally does call at the end of life, blessed will we be!

Wednesday of the Twenty-Ninth Week
of Ordinary Time • Luke 12:39–48

Jesus told his disciples that they must be prepared for and attentive to whatever he required of them. He was concerned with the "R" word: *responsibility*. "Much will be required of the person entrusted with much and still more will be demanded of the person entrusted with more." Being responsible means being attentive to one another.

Even though when people marry, individual freedom is curtailed to a degree, it is when they become parents that being responsible takes on a whole new dimension. Their new child is completely dependent on them. When some people rail against the Catholic Church, usually under all the negative talk lies resentment that something is expected of them. The Lord is clear: With the faith comes responsibility. Elsewhere he said, "Not everyone who says, 'Lord, Lord,' will enter the kingdom of heaven, but those who hear the word of God and keep it."

Thursday of the Twenty-Ninth Week
of Ordinary Time • Luke 12:49–53

Jesus stated that he had come for division. In a household of five, three will be against two, sons against fathers, and mothers against daughters and in-laws against in-laws. He spoke of his Passion as a baptism and said how it anguished him. The division he spoke of is the result of evil in the world. One cannot accommodate evil and at the same time be faithful to him. One must choose!

Nowhere do we see this more blatantly played out than in the abortion problem and other moral situations in which Catholics don't want to take sides for fear of losing an election, or the approval of others, or because they just don't want to bother. His Passion was far more than just a bother. He was motivated by his love and concern for us. What is our motivation? Do we place ourselves first—or him first?

Friday of the Twenty-Ninth Week of Ordinary Time • Luke 12:54–59

Jesus chastised the crowds for their competence in discerning the indications of the weather while they fail to interpret the signs of the times. They had had the preaching of John the Baptist and the teaching of Jesus and still they lived primarily for themselves. They chose not to heed the signs.

We have those same signs in Scripture and the teaching authority of the Church. How much of an impact do they have on the way we live our daily lives? We turn on the Weather Channel or the radio or the computer to check out the weather. But how often do we earnestly seek out the Lord's will for us—with such openness that we put nothing before it, even if it is unpleasant and others may be displeased with us? This isn't always easy, but it's the only response that he deserves!

Saturday of the Twenty-Ninth Week
of Ordinary Time • Luke 13:1–9

When word of the slaughter of some Galileans was presented to Jesus, he brought up the number of people killed by a falling tower in Siloam and warned that far worse would happen to those who would not reform their lives. He then spoke of a fig tree that didn't produce any fruit and how it was decided to give it one more year. If still it didn't bear any fruit, it would be cut down. God was giving Israel great consideration by his presence there. But if it did not respond to this visitation, it would suffer consequences.

So with us, the Lord shows great patience. Left to our own devices—we don't want to be left to our own devices. Without God's help, our lesser selves take over, both personally and collectively. God created us out of nothing. He came first and deserves always to come first.

Thirtieth Sunday of Ordinary Time
Year B • Mark 10:46–52

When a blind man sitting on the side of the road heard that Jesus of Nazareth was about to come by, he began to shout, "Jesus, Son of David, have pity on me!" Many tried to silence him, but he cried out all the more. This was his one chance. A few moments more and Jesus would be gone. He couldn't see where Jesus was. All that was available to him was his voice to cry out with. It boggles my mind why anyone wanted to quiet this poor man. But Jesus heard him and asked how he could help. "I want to see." he said. Jesus replied, "Be on your way! Your faith has healed you." And he was healed and began to follow Jesus. Calling him "Son of David" was a current name for Messiah, so he appears to have had faith.

Heaven begins with an act of faith. And it will grow closer and closer until we see him face to face.

Monday of the Thirtieth Week
of Ordinary Time • Luke 13:10–17

As Jesus laid his hand on a woman who had been bent over for eighteen years, he said, "Woman, you are set free of your infirmity," and she immediately stood erect. Since he cured her on the Sabbath, the indignant synagogue leader told the crowd to come to be cured on any of the day of the week other than the Sabbath. Jesus responded that such officials regularly lead their animals to water on the Sabbath. They therefore were more merciful to the animals than they were to this daughter of Abraham. This simple truth humiliated the synagogue officials and the crowd rejoiced.

Simple truths pass us by when we are in the habit of not living honestly. The lie always demands constant attention for fear of not being consistent. Honest living, on the other hand, is free of such worry because the truth, by its very nature, is one.

Wednesday of the Thirtieth Week
of Ordinary Time • Luke 13:22–30

Someone asked Jesus if only a few people will be saved. He answered by directing him to strive to enter through the narrow gate. Many will try to enter but will not be strong enough. In the kingdom, some who are now last will be first, and some who are now first will be last.

In our culture we are taught to sell ourselves so that we will succeed and beat out the competition. But our Lord turns our culture on its head. Strive to be the least. Defer to others. Our ultimate goal is to love as he loves by sacrificing for each other. We were created for this. Certainly healthy competition is fine for sports and for things that are less important. But for what matters most, we must live our lives in imitation of him who gave his life for the benefit of us all.

Solemnity of All Saints

Thursday of the Thirtieth Week
of Ordinary Time • Matthew 5:1–12a

Jesus taught, "Blessed are the poor in spirit, for theirs is the kingdom of heaven." When he said, "Blessed are they who mourn," "Blessed are the meek," and so on, he was actually speaking of the variety of souls that form the communion of saints, which we celebrate this All Saints Day.

As he was being stoned, St. Stephen forgave his murderers, which included St. Paul. St. John Vianney barely qualified academically for ordination but had half of France coming to him for confession. St. Bernadette didn't know her catechism but was a confidante of the Mother of God. St. Francis of Assisi owned nothing while St. Thomas More had an estate and his own zoo. Harlots and housewives, princes and paupers, janitors and generals—we have all been redeemed by the blood of Christ. How we allow our gratitude to determine the way we live now will determine our future with them in heaven.

Feast of All Souls

Friday of the Thirtieth Week
of Ordinary Time

For today's liturgy on this commemoration of All Souls, the Church's lectionary gives 12 options for the reading of the Gospel. There are so many options because there are so many passages in Scripture that speak about death and eternal life. That is because they are the Gospels' main concern.

Some Christians focus on one or two passages like Romans 10:8: "If you confess with your lips that Jesus is Lord and believe in your heart that God raised him from the dead, you will be saved." True! But salvation demands more. For example: John 3:5: "Unless one is born of water and the Spirit, he cannot enter the kingdom of God." Baptism is necessary for salvation. Or Matthew 7:21: "Not everyone who says to me, 'Lord, Lord,' shall enter the kingdom of heaven, but he who does the will of my Father who is in Heaven." And the most comforting, John 6:54: "He who eats my flesh and drinks my blood has eternal life and I will raise him up on the last day." May our beloved departed rest in peace.

Saturday of the Thirtieth Week
of Ordinary Time • Luke 14:1, 7–11

When dining at the house of a Pharisee, Jesus noticed that so many of the guests were vying for the places of honor at the table. He suggested that taking the lower seat can save embarrassment should one of greater rank be given the place one has already chosen. If one has chosen the lower place, the host can always call him up higher. "For everyone who exalts himself shall be humbled, but the one who humbles himself shall be exalted," he said. Of course the point isn't to make being exalted something to strive for—even if one does so indirectly. The goal is to live honestly. To be honest is to acknowledge the Creator as first. We creatures live to exalt him, which is simply acknowledging him to be who he is. This constitutes worship. To exalt ourselves instead is not only dishonest it is futile. It goes against who we are. We were created to worship at his altar, not ours.

Thirty-First Sunday of Ordinary Time
Year B • Mark 12:28b–34

A scribe asked Jesus which of all the commandments is first. Jesus then recited the *shema*, a prayer that Jews even to the present day recite twice daily, "Hear, O Israel! The Lord our God is Lord alone! Therefore, you shall love the Lord your God with all your heart, with all your soul, with all your mind, and with all your strength." Then he added, "This is the second, 'You shall love your neighbor as yourself.'" The scribe responded, "Excellent, teacher" and went on to praise the answer. Jesus approved of his response, and said, "You are not far from the reign of God." The passage ends with: "And no one had the courage to ask him any more questions." Now why do you suppose that is? When do we not have the courage to learn more about what God may want of us? Usually, it's when we're afraid he may want more from us than we are comfortable with. This would be good to pursue today, don't you think?

Tuesday of the Thirty-First Week
of Ordinary Time • Luke 14:15–24

Jesus told of a man who gave a great dinner, but many of the guests declined to attend for one excuse or another. To take their places, the man commanded his servant to go to the streets and alleys and even the highways to bring people in.

In this parable, Jesus was not only referring to the Jews who were turning their backs on him; he was speaking of anyone he has personally invited to the intimacy of his friendship who has preferred not to partake. How often have we turned our backs on him? Even though he rules the universe, our gift of faith is by way of his personal invitation. He loves us one by one. Notice how impersonally we sin; we don't want to think of him in a personal way when we betray him. Yet his love for us is always personal. It's as individual as the breath he gives us at this very moment.

Wednesday of the Thirty-First Week of Ordinary Time • Luke 14:25–33

When Jesus said, "If anyone comes to me without hating his father and mother, wife and children, brothers and sisters and even his own life, he cannot be my disciple," he was not actually telling us to hate. He was emphasizing that his disciples must absolutely prefer him to everyone and to everything. Many have just passed over such words. Then they become irate when the Church doesn't give way to their desire to live without moral restrictions!

For example: To be his disciple means living as a celibate if one is not married. To knowingly live otherwise is to put ourselves first—not him. "But he can't reasonably expect such deprivation!" some say. Well, we can't have it both ways. We can't accept his sacrificial love and not offer our own in response. He has shown us that sacrifice, not indulgence, is the measure of love.

Thursday of the Thirty-First Week
of Ordinary Time • Luke 15:1–10

The Pharisees disapproved of the attention that Jesus gave to tax collectors and sinners. Jesus responded by asking who among them with a hundred sheep would not leave the 99 to search for one of them that was lost—and then rejoice over finding it. He said that there will be a similar rejoicing before the angels over one repentant sinner.

They didn't understand what he was saying. It never dawned on them that God could be so forgiving and attentive to human weakness. That he would join the human race and suffer and die for it was simply unthinkable. Yet that is precisely what he came to do.

Even we who believe can have considerable difficulty accepting that he loves us that much. That's why it does us well to meditate on the crucifix daily. There *is* rejoicing when we repent!

Feast of the Dedication of the
Basilica of St. John Lateran

Friday of the Thirty-First Week
of Ordinary Time • John 2:13–22

Jesus made a whip out of cords and drove out the venders of animals for temple sacrifice, overturning tables and spilling their contents, ordering them to stop making a marketplace of his Father's house. Nowhere else in the Gospels do we see him so angry.

Through the centuries the Catholic Church has recognized the sacredness of her churches as edifices of worship. Worship is our highest human expression because it is the acknowledgment of who God is. Our churches are sacred places and exist to acknowledge his sovereignty above all else. We don't to go to church to make ourselves feel good. We go to church humbly to acknowledge him and his greatest self-revelation: his Passion and death made evident as we receive his body and blood from the altar at Mass.

Saturday of the Thirty-First Week
of Ordinary Time • Luke 16:9–15

Jesus instructs his listeners that they are to use this world's goods in light of the next world. He doesn't condemn wealth and actually suggests that they make friends with it—while recognizing its seductiveness. "No servant can serve two masters. . . . You cannot give yourself to God and money." The Pharisees, who could be quite avaricious, derided him for this. But he responded, "You justify yourselves in the eyes of men, but God reads your hearts. What man thinks important, God holds in contempt."

How healthy is our attitude toward what we possess? Has there ever been a time when we have been satisfied with what we have? It's worth thinking about.

Thirty-Second Sunday of Ordinary Time
Year B • Mark 12:38–44

Taking a seat opposite the treasury, Jesus noticed people putting money into the collection box. While many of the wealthy put sizable sums into the box, one poor widow put in two small copper coins, worth about a cent. He called his disciples over and told them, "I want you to observe that this poor widow contributed more than all the others. . . . " They had contributed out of their surplus, while she gave all she had to live on. It has always been this way. The poor are always the most generous.

Why do you suppose this is? Wealth does things to us. We immediately begin to worry about losing it, so we tend to hold on to it more. The poor are used to not having and don't tend to obsess on what they have. I know people who readily admit that they were the happiest when they had little. Yet now that they are comfortable, they aren't about to choose to be poor again. What do you think?

Tuesday of the Thirty-Second Week
of Ordinary Time • Luke 17:7–10

Jesus asked his apostles if they would heap praise on a servant for simply doing what he is expected to do. He was concerned that they not become bloated with pride.

Occasionally, confessors have to deal with people who talk about how good they are without any mention of sin. "I haven't murdered anybody. I love my family. I go to Mass." As far as they are concerned, they just don't sin. Actually, it's not uncommon for most of us not to remember any sins. As a good rule of thumb, how frequently do we think of the Lord's generosity? We all fall short on this one. Out of sight, out of mind is often our mode unless we're hurting. Considering his time on the cross can bring our self-absorption, pride, and selfishness to mind more quickly than we might think. It is his love that always sets us straight.

Wednesday of the Thirty-Second Week
of Ordinary Time • Luke 17:11–19

On his way through Samaria, Jesus cleansed ten lepers and only one came back to thank him. He then asked. "Has none but this foreigner returned to give thanks?" His countrymen were obviously numb to his generosity. Often when we don't know people well, we are more apt to be open to their qualities because we aren't as likely to measure ourselves against them as we are to those close to us.

When I was novice master I had the novices preach homilies to each other for practice—outside of Mass, of course. When one of them revealed an exceptional ability to preach, one of his classmates blurted out, "He's the best! He's just the best!" Because he wasn't taken up with himself, he could recognize God's gift to another, delight in it, and be grateful for it. While jealously blinds, love helps us to see.

Thursday of the Thirty-Second Week of Ordinary Time • Luke 17:20–25

In answer to the Pharisees, Jesus said, "The coming of the Kingdom of God cannot be observed, and no one will announce, 'Look, here it is,' or, 'There it is.' For behold, the Kingdom of God is among you." In other words, the kingdom of God was already present and the Pharisees weren't aware of it because they were looking for something else.

I'm reminded of a cartoon of two fleas walking on a dog's back among the hairs that look like towering trees next to them. One of them said, "Sometimes I doubt if there really is a dog!" The kingdom of God is all around us, as Good Friday so eloquently announces. Moment by moment we each have the opportunity to affirm it or deny it by affirming or denying the king. We adore you, O Christ, and we praise you. By your holy cross you have redeemed the world.

Saturday of the Thirty-Second Week
of Ordinary Time • Luke 18:1–8

Jesus spoke of an unscrupulous judge who was hounded by a widow who demanded he give her justice over her opponent. For a time he refused, but because her unremitting insistence was wearing him out, he settled in her favor. He then suggested that if such a corrupt judge will do justice to those who call out to him night and day, how much more will a loving God! How many times after he had healed a person of some malady did Jesus tell them that it was their faith that healed them? Faith and humility were the two attributes he continually responded to. We certainly see these in the saints, beginning with our Blessed Mother. She never wavered in her trust in God—even though over and over she didn't understand what he was asking. She just said yes and trusted him. Now she's someone to keep company with today.

Thirty-Third Sunday of Ordinary Time
Year B • Mark 13:24–32

We read about the last things and the Second Coming of Christ to earth. Can Advent be far? Actually, it's only two weeks away—already. In this season, we begin our celebration of the First Coming of the Lord. At the end of the liturgical year, we consider the last days. It all fits together. The story of our salvation is the story of a loving God and his creatures, who need him even to be able to love him. It contains metaphorical descriptions of the sun darkening and the stars falling. As to the exact day or hour, no one knows except the Father.

But practically, our own death is our own last day, when we will receive God's judgment privately. We're all terminal. It's just a matter of time. It's a good reason for us to daily submit our lives to him who sacrificed his life for ours.

Monday of the Thirty-Third Week
of Ordinary Time • Luke 18:35–43

When a blind man sitting by the roadside heard that Jesus was passing by he immediately began to shout, "Jesus, Son of David, have pity on me!" When others tried to silence him, he cried out all the louder. He knew that in a matter of moments and a few steps, Jesus would have gone, never to return. This was his one chance.

Do we ever pray like that? Is it ever that important to us that Jesus hear us? Jesus did indeed hear him and asked what he wanted. "Lord, please, that I may see!" Jesus immediately gave him sight and told him that his faith had saved him—thereby telling him that his confidence in Jesus was the greater gift. How much confidence do we have in him? Do we trust his love for us? Or, blinded by our egos, do we fail to see?

Tuesday of the Thirty-Third Week
of Ordinary Time • Luke 19:1–10

In Jericho, Zachaeus, a wealthy tax collector, climbed a sycamore tree in order to see Jesus. Jesus called him down by name and stayed at his house, to the dismay of many in the crowd. But there on the spot Zachaeus committed half his wealth to the poor and resolved to pay fourfold anyone he may have extorted. Our Lord responded, "Today salvation has come to this house."

It was the Lord's grace that touched Zachaeus and he chose to accept it. It was personal and immediate. Recently I received an inquiry from a soldier in Iraq who noticed the old prayer to St. Michael the Archangel taped to a Humvee. It piqued his interest to such a degree that he investigated the Catholic Church and plans to join it. Our faith comes to us as personally and uniquely as it did to the man on the sycamore tree. Zachaeus is you and me.

Wednesday of the Thirty-Third Week
of Ordinary Time • Luke 19:11–28

Jesus told of a nobleman who gave 10 gold coins to his 10 servants before leaving on a long trip. Upon his arrival home, he checked with each servant, and all but one had earned additional coins. The one who horded the coins, blinded by fear, didn't even bank them for interest.

I'm reminded of the six-year-old boy who had several toys out in the back yard when a friend of his father arrived with his four-year-old son. The younger boy immediately began playing with the toys. The older boy watched, and when the younger boy left one toy for another, he put each one in the garage until they were all accounted for. He then closed the door, snapped the padlock, and went into the house. Here again we see some hording, along with some passive aggression and much control. With some it starts early. What we do not see is the magnanimity the Lord asks of us.

It's been many years since that day, and I'm still working on it.

Thanksgiving Day

Thursday of the Thirty-Third Week of Ordinary Time • Luke 17:11–19

When Jesus cured 10 lepers and only one of them came back, threw himself on his face at the feet of Jesus, and honored him, Jesus said to him, "Stand up, your faith has been your salvation."

So often our Lord identifies people's gratitude with faith, and it makes perfect sense. The greatest gifts we have we only know by faith. Certainly the greatest gift we have is Good Friday. But without faith, it's just another day. How many with faith on this Thanksgiving Day will think to give thanks for his Passion and death? Make no mistake about it: His Passion and death is the greatest act of love we will ever know here on earth. What a gift! It is by far our greatest possession. At least in our hearts, let us fall on our faces in homage and give thanks for it.

Friday of the Thirty-Third Week
of Ordinary Time • Luke 19:45–48

Jesus entered the temple area and drove out those who were selling things. The chief priests and scribes saw him daily teaching in the temple and were seeking ways to put him to death. But they were continually thwarted in this because the people hung on his words.

Through the centuries this has been the case with some and not with others. The chief priests and scribes certainly never hung on his words. Yet a tax collector named Matthew did and eventually wrote many of them down. It's all a matter of his grace and our willingness to accept it. Jesus said that no one comes to him unless the Father draws him. Do you feel the pull? I certainly do—even on a shopping day as busy as this one. His grace is everywhere and his word is life!

Saturday of the Thirty-Third Week
of Ordinary Time • Luke 20:27–40

Some Sadducees, who didn't believe in the resurrection of the dead, posed a question to Jesus about a widow whose seven husbands all died before her. When she eventually died, whose wife would she be? Jesus undercut their attempt to trap him by explaining that heaven is so different from what we know. There, we are all children of a loving God. Actually, all sacraments are fulfilled by our union with God—which is what heaven is. Sometimes people will ask if they will still be united to their spouses in heaven. The answer is that they will be united with everyone in heaven in a bond that is beyond anything they knew on earth. So, yes, they will still be united with their spouses—plus many more!

Feast of Christ the King

Thirty-Fourth Sunday of Ordinary Time
Year B • John 18:33b–37

When Pilate enquired of Jesus if he was a king, he answered, "My kingdom does not belong to this world. If my kingdom were of this world, my subjects would be fighting to save me from being handed over to the Jews. As it is, my kingdom is not here." So Pilate responded, "So, then, you are a king?" Jesus replied, "It is you who say I am a king. The reason I was born, the reason why I came into the world, is to testify to the truth. Anyone committed to the truth hears my voice."

Here on the last Sunday of the liturgical year, after we have gone through the whole life of Jesus on earth, we find ourselves in the middle of the Passion because we have never really left it. It remains the center of liturgical focus because it is the center of our lives. Our king wore a crown of thorns. Our God allowed himself to be put to death by his creatures, making possible our eternity with him. It is the truth. Do you hear his voice?

Monday of the Thirty-Fourth Week
of Ordinary Time • Luke 21:1–4

As he saw the rich putting their gifts into the temple treasury, Jesus noticed a poor widow putting in two small copper coins. He then said that she had put in more than all the rest because they had given from their surplus, but she gave all that she had to live on.

Contrast this with the audiences that tune in each week to reality TV programs in which people compete for positions of prestige and wealth. Our culture is so bent on the self and any kind of instant gratification—whether it is the desire for power and status or the desires of the flesh—that it needs ever stronger stimuli to be satisfied. St. Augustine astutely reminded us that our hearts are restless until they rest in the Lord. Our very restless world will remain so until it prefers nothing to Christ.

Wednesday of the Thirty-Fourth Week of Ordinary Time • Luke 21:12–19

Jesus warned his disciples that they would eventually be brought before hostile kings and governors and would be betrayed by relatives and friends. However, they were not to worry about what to say. Not a hair of their heads would perish. This, of course, presupposed their loyalty.

Sometimes it is much easier to give witness to him to people we don't know than to those who are close to us—especially our own families. The loss of our family's friendship and approval can be quite painful and awkward, especially on family days such as the holidays. He knows what this is like. Remember him standing in disgrace at the praetorium with the crowds calling for his Crucifixion, and no one—no one—defended him?

When we speak his truth to those whose rejection can hurt, we are at the praetorium, kneeling in adoration before him.

Thursday of the Thirty-Fourth Week
of Ordinary Time • Luke 21:20–28

Jesus warns his disciples of the final days. "There will be signs in the sun, the moon and the stars, and on earth nations will be in anguish, perplexed by the roaring of the sea and the waves. . . . And then they will see the Son of Man coming in a cloud with power and great glory. But when these signs begin to happen, stand erect and raise your hands because your redemption is at hand."

There have been many who have erroneously announced that day and time. Yet our Lord has explicitly stipulated that no one but the Father knows the day or the hour of the general judgment. But the individual judgment awaits each of us when we die. This is the one we need to be prepared for at every moment. Let us live with our eyes of faith wide open, always attentive to his will, and we will be ready.

Feast of St. Andrew, Apostle

Friday of the Thirty-Fourth Week
of Ordinary Time • Matthew 4:18–22

As Jesus walked by the Sea of Galilee, he called to Peter and his brother Andrew, "Come after me and I will make you fishers of men." Unlike this and the other synoptic Gospels, the Gospel of John describes Andrew as one of John the Baptist's disciples who was so taken with Jesus that he went and told his brother Peter about him. What was it about Jesus that so attracted him? Certainly the Baptist deferred to him, calling him the Lamb of God. What is it about him that attracts us? Well, it's grace at work in our souls that attracts us—the same grace that drew Andrew to follow him. It also brought him to the X-shaped cross that he died on.

It is by the cross that Jesus calls everyone. It is through the crosses in our lives that we demonstrate our love for him.

DECEMBER 1, 2012

Saturday of the Thirty-Fourth Week
of Ordinary Time • Luke 21:34–36

Jesus told his disciples to be on guard lest their spirits become bloated with indulgence and drunkenness and worldly cares. He said that the great day will suddenly close in on them like a trap. It will come upon all on the face of the earth. So they were to pray constantly. All the apostles were martyred except for John, who died of natural causes. But the warnings still apply for us. For those who are faithful to him, the day will not find them unprepared.

But for those who refuse to take such warnings seriously, they have reason to stop and take stock of their lives and the direction they are going. His mercy is limitless, but only for those who ask for it. Now is the time.

First Sunday of Advent • Year C
Luke 21:25–28, 34–36

Jesus told his disciples that there will be signs in the sun, the moon, and the stars. Nations will be in anguish. The powers in the heavens will be shaken. Then the Son of Man will come on a cloud with great power and glory. The great day will come suddenly upon all who dwell on earth. He encouraged them to pray constantly for strength to escape whatever is in the future and to stand secure before the Son of Man.

The key phrase here is "come suddenly." The Second Coming of the Lord will not be expected. The signs in the skies will not precede but will accompany and be a part of the final event. There will be no warning—other than this one. It is up to us to submit to the love we find on Calvary and remain faithful at all times.

First Monday of Advent • Matthew 8:5–11

When Jesus responded to a centurion's request that he help his paralyzed servant, the centurion said that he was not worthy to have Jesus enter under his roof, but to simply say the word and the man would be healed.

"I too am a man subject to authority with men subject to me," he said, referring to the power he had over them. Jesus was most impressed with this Roman pagan, who acknowledged Jesus' relationship to the Father and his supernatural power—to which the Jews were oblivious.

Even today his words endure in our liturgy: "Lord, I am not worthy that you should enter under my roof, but only say the word and my soul shall be healed." It is a continual reminder that what matters most is the kind of humility and faith the centurion had, the love that Jesus has for us—and our willingness to make such humility and faith our own.

First Tuesday of Advent • Luke 10:21–24

Jesus rejoiced in the Holy Spirit and said, "I give you praise, Father, Lord of heaven and earth, for although you have hidden these things from the wise and learned, you have revealed them to the childlike."

Aren't you glad that you are not wise and learned? What would your life be like if the Gospel had never been revealed to you? What would your understanding of death be? What would you live for? What would be the meaning of your life?

"Blessed are the eyes that see what you see," he said. "Many prophets have longed to see what you see but did not see it and to hear what you hear and did not hear it." Just think of the comfort and strength we receive from the sacraments! We have such sight and knowledge only through the faith that has been given to us. We have much need to rejoice in the Holy Spirit as well!

First Wednesday of Advent
Matthew 15:29–37

From a mountainside near the Sea of Galilee, Jesus cured the lame, the mute, and the blind. He told his disciples, "My heart is moved with pity for the crowd, for they have been with me now for three days and have nothing to eat." So from a few fish and five loaves of bread he miraculously fed the crowds, with seven baskets of food left over.

Surely, most of us have been with him for more than three days. Daily he feeds all our needs. Yet we tend to dwell on what we don't have and still want—without regard for our lack of gratitude. We seldom think of ourselves as being ungrateful—yet most of our thoughts are all about us. Conversion means centering on him instead of ourselves. Let's make sure that today we thank him for who he is and for our awareness of him!

First Thursday of Advent
Matthew 7:21, 24–27

Jesus told his disciples, "Not everyone who says to me, 'Lord, Lord,' will enter the Kingdom of heaven, but only the one who does the will of my Father in heaven." This is what the Catholic Church means by acknowledging the need for good works.

While our salvation is the sole result of God's benevolent grace, something is expected of us. We must listen to his words and act on them. So we are to pray daily, feed the hungry, encourage the faint-hearted, care for the sick, visit those in prison, and share the good news with whoever is willing to hear us. If we are unwilling to do these things, we will not enter the kingdom of heaven—no matter how strong our original conversion fervor happened to be. We have the Lord's word on it: Doing the will of the Father is necessary for us to enter the kingdom of heaven.

First Friday of Advent • Matthew 9:27–31

As Jesus passed two blind men, they cried out, "Son of David, have pity on us!" He asked them if they believed that he could heal them and they responded "yes." He then touched their eyes and they could see. He warned them not to tell anyone, but they spread the word about it to all.

Would you have been able to keep quiet about such a thing? I probably would not have been able to. Yet we have better news even than that. How often do we realize this? And why aren't we eager to spread the word about it?

He has done far more for us than giving us physical sight. He has given us the hope of eternal life with him. Unlike those blind men, we don't realize what spiritual blindness is like, and so are not appreciative of the light we can see. We can see it. It is a gift. It is ours!

Solemnity of the
Immaculate Conception of Mary

First Saturday of Advent • Luke 1:26–38

God sent the angel Gabriel to Mary with the words, "Hail, full of grace! The Lord is with you." Today we celebrate these words and what they mean. Grace is that supernatural gift from God that makes us his children—members of his family, if you will, inheritors of his kingdom. For us, this grace comes to us in baptism, because each of us is born with the effects of Adam's original sin. But Mary, according to Scripture, was full of grace and therefore could have no sin within her.

Why this is so brings us to consider who her Son is. Jesus is both human and divine. For the Son of God to take flesh from a human being, tainted with sin, would be an affront to his divinity. So Mary was preserved from original sin on his behalf. In acknowledging that she was immaculately conceived, we actually honor him.

Second Sunday of Advent • Year C
Luke 3:1–6

We find a rather formal introduction of John the Baptist. Since Luke is writing for a Gentile audience, he doesn't mention John's diet or other details that would detract from the baptism and introduction of Jesus. "In the fiftieth year of the rule of Tiberius Caesar, when Pontius Pilate was procurator of Judea"—and he mentions all the various pertinent leaders of the day—"the word of God was spoken to John son of Zechariah in the desert." It then speaks of John going about the region of the Jordan proclaiming a baptism of repentance that led to the forgiveness of sins as described by the prophet Isaiah.

This sounds rather remote from us in our own current situation, yet it bears directly on the meaning of our lives. As John introduces Jesus to the world, he introduces the salvation on which our lives depend in every beat of our hearts.

Second Monday of Advent
Luke 5:17–26

Some men brought in a paralyzed man on stretcher and lowered him down through the tiles in the ceiling because of the crowd. Jesus then told the man, "As for you, your sins are forgiven." To the scribes and Pharisees he said, "What are you thinking in your hearts? Which is easier to say, 'Your sins are forgiven,' or 'Rise and walk'?" Then he told the man to pick up his stretcher and walk—which he did, to everyone's amazement.

What are you thinking in your heart as you hear this? What is it that you want him to heal or to change: family upheaval, illness, a sexual difficulty, a mental problem? He can do this. But looking at eternity, which is of the most value? Removing your current cross or the forgiveness of your sins? Sometimes thinking inside the box is the most rewarding—when it's a confessional box!

Second Tuesday of Advent
Matthew 18:12–14

Jesus speaks of the shepherd who leaves his herd in search of a stray sheep. When he finds it, he rejoices more over it than over those that had not strayed. In just the same way, it is the will of the Father that not one of his little ones be lost.

Believe it or not, he's speaking of you and me. Compared with him, we're pretty small potatoes. We are his little ones. This is why it is so necessary for us to keep our attention on who he is. Without that perspective, we begin to think we are more important than we are, and this gets us into big trouble. When we recognize how generous he is and how much greater he is than we are, our gratitude makes us humble and we don't lose sight of who we are. It is at such moments that we are most pleasing to him—not to mention those around us.

Feast of Our Lady of Guadalupe

Second Wednesday of Advent
Luke 1:26–38

When the angel Gabriel appeared to Mary, saying, "Hail, full of grace! The Lord is with you," she was greatly troubled by his words.

Centuries later, in 1531, as a woman with child she appeared to Juan Diego at Tepeyac, Mexico. He was no less troubled by her visit than she had been with the angel. But her simple ways immediately put him at ease. At 57 years old he was considered elderly at the time. So he referred to her as "My Child, the most tender of my daughters" while she referred to him as "My son the least." Only the humble can fully appreciate each other. She visited one of those considered the least among us, and he, at her bidding, built a shrine where other such souls would know God's love for them for generations to come. And so the Feast of Our Lady of Guadalupe came to pass.

Second Thursday of Advent
Matthew 11:11–15

Jesus said to the crowds, "Amen, I say to you, among those born of women there has been none greater than John the Baptist; yet the least in the Kingdom of heaven is greater than he." John was the last of the Old Testament prophets.

In speaking of Jesus, he had said, "I must decrease that he may increase." Like St. Joseph, he was glad to work in the background in preparation for the Redeemer. But for the Lord there is only foreground. No loving deed ever passes unnoticed by him. He tells us to pray in secret—not that he doesn't expect us to pray together also. But prayer in secret is intimate and not for the eyes of anyone but him. Each one of us needs to pray daily in this way. Our private self is who we really are. Find a quiet spot in your day. You have words that need to be said to him and he has words for you as well.

Second Friday of Advent
Matthew 11:16–19

Jesus said, "To what shall I compare this generation?" He then compared it to children who antagonize each other with expectations that are impossible to fulfill. John the Baptist fasted and abstained from wine and they said he was possessed by a demon. Jesus came eating and drinking and they called him a glutton and drunkard.

But wisdom is vindicated by its works. Jesus was always concerned about reality and not about how things appeared—and he still is! Talk is cheap. Jesus came eating and drinking; he also suffered and died on the cross for us, where his words are vindicated and heaven has been opened to us. The lover is the one who is willing to sacrifice. He designed us to be lovers, to put ourselves out for others. That's how we know we love them!

Second Saturday of Advent
Matthew 17:9a, 10–13

Coming down the mountain after having seen Jesus transfigured before them, the disciples asked him why the scribes said that Elijah must come first. He answered that Elijah had already come, but they didn't recognize him and did as they pleased. When he said that the Son of Man would also suffer at their hands, the disciples understood that he was speaking of John the Baptist.

Just as the Baptist had suffered a seemingly senseless death as the result of evil, so would Jesus and the disciples. The disciples had no idea of the martyrdom they were to endure, nor of the love that would give them triumph. This is why the Lord allows such evil and the reason for the crosses we have in our lives. Whatever crosses he has planned for us, we can know that if we carry them faithfully, his triumph awaits us.

Third Sunday of Advent • Year C
Luke 3:10–18

In response to his preaching that they reform their lives, the people asked John the Baptist what they ought to do. He told them to share their goods with those who were without. Tax collectors were to exact nothing over their fixed amount. Soldiers were not to bully or denounce falsely and they were to be content with their pay. They were to live honestly. The people were quite taken with John, but he assured them that there was one mightier than he who was to come, whose sandal strap he was not worthy to loosen. He would baptize with fire and the Holy Spirit.

Many of us have been baptized with the Holy Spirit and know the one of whom John spoke. How honestly do we live?

Third Monday of Advent
Matthew 1:1–17

The Gospel of Matthew begins with the genealogy of Jesus, since Matthew was particularly concerned with his Jewish audience and their sensibilities. It provided Jesus' background and family history. Knowing where someone came from—their context—throws a light on who the person really is.

What is your context? Now, you could tell me about your ethnic background and your city of birth and your upbringing. You could mention your parents' education and occupations. You could mention your own education and occupation. You could even name your ancestors. But none of these is really necessary. All you need do is tell me that you are a Catholic. By this I will know that your context is Jesus Christ and the Church he founded. This is who you are.

Third Tuesday of Advent
Matthew 1:18–24

When Mary was found to be with child, Joseph decided to divorce her quietly to prevent her from suffering public shame. An angel then appeared to him in his sleep, telling him not to fear taking Mary as his wife—that it was by the Holy Spirit that she had conceived.

When he awoke, he took her home as his wife. The Gospel says, "He had no relations with her until she bore a son and he named him Jesus." Note, the word *until* does not always suggest that something is to follow. It can also mean up to a point and no further, as when one says, "He was faithful until he died." Certainly we don't mean that he was unfaithful after he died. Likewise Joseph had no relations with Mary until and after the birth of Jesus. The rest of his life continued to be distinguished by his complete submission to God's sovereignty over him. May we follow his lead!

Third Wednesday of Advent
Luke 1:5–25

While the priest Zechariah entered the sanctuary to burn incense, the angel Gabriel appeared to him, telling him that his barren wife would bear him a son who would be filled with the Holy Spirit and would bring many Israelites to the Lord. He questioned how this could be since he and his wife were advanced in years. Gabriel replied that he would be unable to speak until the day that this prophecy was fulfilled because he had doubted. When Zechariah emerged from the sanctuary, he was unable to speak, and the people realized that he had seen a vision. Shortly thereafter his wife, Elizabeth, conceived in her old age.

God had a purpose in not giving them children through all the years. How many days had they wondered why their prayers seemed not to have been heard! God always has a plan. It is for us to acknowledge his sovereignty by trusting him—and thereby show our love for him.

Third Thursday of Advent
Luke 1:26–38

The angel Gabriel greeted Mary with the words, "Hail, full of grace! The Lord is with you." He then cautioned her not to fear, that she had found favor with God and was to conceive in her womb a son to be named Jesus. By the Holy Spirit she would miraculously conceive a child who would be the Son of God.

Unlike Zechariah, Mary did not doubt the angel—even though this message was even more extraordinary than the one he received. Her humility *that* won the day. No one else has ever been greeted as being full of grace—not "highly favored" one, as some mistranslations state. Some ask where Scripture says that she was immaculately conceived. Here it is: To be full of grace is to have no—absolutely no—evidence of sin whatsoever. Immaculate, humble, holy, and the Mother of God—this is who she is!

Third Friday of Advent
Luke 1:39–45

Mary set out to the town of Judah where she entered Zechariah's house and greeted Elizabeth. When Elizabeth heard Mary's voice, the child in her womb leaped for joy, and filled with the Holy Spirit she exclaimed, "Blessed are you among women and blessed is the fruit of your womb. How is it that the mother of my Lord should come to me?"

No two human beings have ever had such a meeting! This meeting of two women is unparalleled in the history of the human race. As exalted as this feminine communication is, it goes unnoted by most feminists. It requires faith to appreciate fully. To look at these two women so highly endowed by the Holy Spirit is to be grateful for their lives, which touch our own lives so deeply. We are therefore humbled by their generous hearts and their love for God.

Third Saturday of Advent
Luke 1:46–56

Elizabeth asks Mary, "Who am I that the mother of my Lord should come to me?" Mary responds that her soul magnifies the Lord. Her spirit rejoices in God, her Savior.

She begins by deferring to God, emphasizing that there is no reason to congratulate her since it has all been his doing. Her good fortune lies in the fact that he noticed one as insignificant as she. She acknowledges God as her Savior and in so doing acknowledges her need for the salvation her Son would bring. As a child of Adam, she needed the preventive grace that saved her from incurring the stain of both original and actual sins. The purity of her humility and integrity shows as clear as a spotless window. Surely the gift of her Son came to us in a precious gift as well.

Fourth Sunday of Advent • Year C
Luke 1:39–45

Mary set out in haste to the hill country where she greeted her relative Elizabeth. When Elizabeth heard her, the baby in her womb leapt for joy. Elizabeth, filled with the Holy Spirit, cried out, "Blessed are you among women and blessed is the fruit of your womb. But who am I that the mother of my Lord should come to me?" While the whole earth was oblivious to this meeting, heaven rejoiced that God was, at last, visiting his people in a most remarkable way. The word had become flesh and these two women, who seemed so insignificant, were divinely favored beyond human imagining.

And yet we share in such favor to the degree that we believe. The gift of faith is no less deliberately given and we are no less divinely favored. The favor is Christ's gift of himself.

Fourth Monday of Advent
Luke 1:67–79

As the Holy Spirit came upon John the Baptist's father, Zechariah, he exclaimed, "Blessed be the Lord, the God of Israel, for he has come to his people and set them free." He had not believed the angel who had announced to him that his wife would conceive in her old age and that their son would prepare the way for the coming of the Messiah. He was therefore made mute until what he was told came to pass. Now it had, and as his son was circumcised, his tongue was loosened, and he could again speak.

Over and over Scripture reminds us how important it is to trust the Lord and have faith in him. Our faith is the most powerful gift we have. It is also the most precious. Certainly, it is the preeminent Christmas gift, because it gives us access to Christ himself.

Solemnity of Christmas

John 1:1–18

John begins his Gospel with "In the beginning was the Word." He leaves no doubt about the divinity of Jesus and that as God he has always existed and that it was through him that the Father created all things.

So why did he choose to take on our human nature and suffer and die for the creatures he authored? It was not simply to inspire people to give gifts to each other in a spirit of family feeling and good will to all. No— he came as a remedy for sin. His presence among us, from the poverty in which he was born to the agony in which he died, was also to demonstrate the divine love our Triune God has for us, and then to enable us to imitate that love in a way that we could never achieve on our own. This is the glory of Christmas! It is the glory of Jesus Christ in human history and the glory of your life and mine.

Feast of St. Stephen, Deacon and Martyr

Wednesday in the Octave of Christmas
Matthew 10:17–22

Jesus warned his disciples not to worry about what to say in the face of opposition. "The Spirit of your Father will be speaking in you," he said. "You will be hated by all on account of me. But whoever holds out to the end will escape death."

Today we celebrate the deacon Stephen, who witnessed to Jesus. The Gospel says that his words stung his listeners to the heart. They ground their teeth in anger against him and rushed at him as one man. As he was being stoned, he prayed for them as he gave his spirit up to the Lord. As in the case of his Lord, his death was a triumph. Saul, who stood by approving of his martyrdom, was to become Paul, the apostle to the Gentiles, and one day would meet him in heaven.

We Christians are not perfect; we are simply sinners who can be transformed by God's love.

Feast of St. John, Apostle and Evangelist

Thursday in the Octave of Christmas
John 20:1a, 2–8

On Easter morning Peter and John ran to the tomb where Jesus was laid. John arrived first but deferred to Peter to enter. Peter observed the cloths that Jesus had been wrapped in. When John entered, the Gospel says that he saw and believed.

Of all the disciples, he alone was at the cross when Jesus died. His fear had evidently been overcome by his concern for the women, especially the Mother of Jesus. His was the unique honor of giving solace to her and therefore to Jesus. He was close enough to have been spattered by the blood. His was the sorrow of seeing his master die. So when he saw the cloths, and saw that the body of Jesus was gone, he believed. A week later he had the joy of seeing Jesus, risen from the dead. Today we honor this holy evangelist. St. John, pray for us who also believe.

Feast of the Holy Innocents

Friday in the Octave of Christmas
Matthew 2:13–18

King Herod, furious at being deceived by the astrologers, ordered the massacre of all little boys of two years and younger in Bethlehem and its surroundings. We have come to call these children the Holy Innocents. Today we honor them as saints.

Often people ask if a baby who dies without being baptized will go to heaven. The *Catechism of the Catholic Church* recalls God's desire that all be saved, as well as the great love Jesus had for children. This allows us to hope that such children are at home in heaven. It is also good to note that the Holy Innocents were not, technically speaking, martyrs, as they had no choice in the matter. They certainly were not baptized and still we recognize that they are in heaven. May the thousands of innocents who are the victims of abortion be among them.

Saturday in the Octave of Christmas
Luke 2:22–35

Mary and Joseph took the baby Jesus to Jerusalem according to the Old Law to present him to the Lord. When the holy man Simeon saw them, he was overwhelmed. Taking the baby in his arms, he exclaimed, "Lord, now let your servant go in peace; your word has been fulfilled: my own eyes have seen the salvation which you have prepared in the sight of every people, a light to reveal you to the nations and the glory of your people Israel."

As Simeon closes his life with these words, the Church in the Liturgy of the Hours appropriately closes each day with these words, at the final liturgical hour known as Compline, which means completion. None of us has the assurance that we will live through the night. At day's end we ought to take stock of our behavior during the day and repent of any wrongdoing as we commend ourselves to him whom we love and live for.

Feast of the Holy Family

Sunday in the Octave of Christmas
Year C • Luke 2:41–52

Mary and Joseph took Jesus, who was now 12 years old, to Jerusalem for Passover. After a day's journey on their return home, they realized that Jesus was not with them. So they returned to Jerusalem to search for him. After three days of worry, they found him in the temple, sitting in the midst of the teachers, asking questions. When they conveyed their worry and frustration, he responded, "Did you not know that I had to be in my Father's house?" Luke writes that they did not understand what he said to them. But they did understand that as accustomed as they were to his ways, there was much more about him that they did not and could not know. He went home and was obedient to them. But as the days passed, they were to see more and more what a marvel he was.

The more time *we* spend with him, the more *we* will see what a marvel he is as well.

Monday in the Octave of Christmas
John 1:1–18

We see that God the Father created all that is, through Jesus, the Word. Jesus designed the very ones he was to redeem. So we were born with our genetic makeup by his design. Let's remember this the next time we complain because we don't have the natural gifts that others may have. We are the way we naturally are by his design. I remember as a child being so intimidated by people who were whizzes at math because I was so poor at it. Later I learned that he never wanted me to be a whiz at math. He wanted me to appreciate that gift in others. There was no need to be intimidated.

But the best part is that he loves what he designed in the way he designed it—as he demonstrated on Good Friday. As John says, "From his fullness we have all received grace in place of grace."